HOW TO INVEST $50-$5000

NANCY DUNNAN

BARNES & NOBLE BOOKS
A DIVISION OF HARPER & ROW, PUBLISHERS
New York, Cambridge, Philadelphia, San Francisco
London, Mexico City, São Paulo, Sydney

Produced by Cloverdale Press, Inc. 133 Fifth Avenue, New York, NY 10003

HOW TO INVEST $50–$5,000. Copyright © 1985 by Cloverdale Press Inc. All rights reserved. Printed in the United States of America. No part of this book may be used or reproduced in any manner whatsoever without written permission except in the case of brief quotations embodied in critical articles and reviews. For information address Harper & Row, Publishers, Inc., 10 East 53rd Street, New York, N.Y. 10022.

FIRST EDITION

Library of Congress Cataloging in Publication Data

Dunnan, Nancy.
  How to invest $50–$5,000.

(The Smart money series)
Includes index.
1. Investments—Handbooks, manuals, etc.   I. Title.   II. Title: How to invest fifty to five thousand dollars.   III. Series.
HG4527.D77   1985   332.6′78   84-48412
ISBN 0-06-464100-7

85 86 87 88 89 10 9 8 7 6 5 4 3 2 1

CONTENTS

PART ONE

Getting the Most for Your Money

 # Introduction

The glitter of gold, the headiness of interest rates, the cooling of inflation, and a significant spurt in the economy have infused all of us, whether we're timid or assertive when it comes to money matters, with an intense desire to take home a piece of the action. In fact, the current lure of investing has never been greater; for every month during the past ten years, 500,000 new investors have opened some type of account. Not all of them stay in the market, but most do.

According to a recent study, the average new investor is thirty-four years old, female, with $2,200 to invest. Her first move, typically, is to purchase an IRA, or Individual Retirement Account. (So should you, incidentally.)

Maybe you, too, are one of these new or small investors, trying to decide just what to do with your money. Or perhaps you've had money sitting in an account somewhere earning 5¼ percent.... Maybe you're just starting out on your first job....Maybe you've saved several hundred dollars from your summer work....or several thousand dollars from careful budgeting....You received a sudden windfall so that for the first time in your life you have a lump sum to invest....You got a bonus....or you have a business that's taking off...

Even if you have only a small amount to invest, you should start now—today; for the sooner you begin, the sooner your $50, $500, or $5,000 will grow. Think about it: If you invested $500 per year at 12 percent compounded annually, at the end of five years you would have $3,175. At the end of ten years you would have $8,775. You too can watch your money grow through wise investment.

Sometimes small investors feel their options are limited. They're not. Over two dozen investment vehicles are described in detail in this book. We will show you how to take advantage of each one. In fact, you'll soon discover that all the financial world is wooing you and your money. Banks, brokerage firms, insurance companies, and financial planners are vying for your cash—be it $50 or $5,000. In fact, every major financial institution has a new gimmick to entice the novice as well as to hold on to the seasoned client.

At the same time, as you may have noticed, investing has become awfully complicated. The line between broker and banker is increasingly blurred as financial supermarkets, or "one-stop" money shopping takes over. Undoubtedly you have read that banks are steadily moving into the world of stocks and money market funds, while brokers, on the other hand, are now selling CDs (Certificates of Deposit). American Express joined Shearson; Sears and Dean Witter are now a twosome; and Prudential Insurance and Bache work in tandem. Each of these and other firms offers a multitude of investment choices, making it all the more difficult to know where to go with your hard-earned money.

We'll explain which ones are best, which ones are safest, which ones will give you the best return. You will learn that a savings account at your corner bank is no longer the only option for the small investor. In this handbook, we will teach you to feel comfortable moving your money around, from one investment to another as your needs change, as interest rates and the economy change. The right place for your first $50 won't be the right one for your first $500 or $5,000.

Those of us with up to $5,000 constitute the nation's largest group of investors, and we are the key target market for the financial institutions. Yet, it's not easy to find information explaining how to tailor personal needs to specific investment instruments. Most money books address people in high-income brackets—those who can afford a financial planner to guide their every move.

This book will change all that for you. It will fill that void by covering the specific concerns of those who have a maximum of $5,000 to invest. It will tackle the fact that in today's climate no one type of investment works well all the time; that reading the changes in interest rates is crucial; that diversification will minimize financial pitfalls; and, finally, that liquidity and the ability to move assets quickly are essential in a changing economic climate.

How to Invest $50 to $5,000 will carefully guide you through the maze of money vehicles, teaching you how to develop the art of smart decision making. You will learn to tackle Wall Street and your bank with confidence and self-assurance. We won't tell you which stock to buy, which bond is best, or even which bank to use, but we will show you how to analyze your options as you watch your money grow from $50 to $5,000. Cutting through the jargon and getting right down to the basic facts, *How to Invest $50 to $5,000* will explain things financial so that no matter how inexperienced you are, you soon will feel comfortable deciding where to put your investment dollars.

Being a good investor, however, takes time and knowledge. But if you follow our step-by-step plan, you'll soon know exactly what to do and when. Make a point of setting aside some time to learn about handling your money, to explore the world of finance. It's worth the time and effort for one simple reason: No one cares as much about your money as you do!

2 Your IRA or Keogh Plan

Without a doubt, the very first $2,000 that you manage to accumulate should be invested in an *IRA* (Individual Retirement Account) or in a *Keogh Plan*. An IRA, just as its name implies, is a tax-advantaged account into which individuals contribute money that is invested for their retirement. A Keogh Plan is a similar tax-advantaged account designed for the self-employed. The money in both accumulates tax-free interest or dividends until you retire or take it out.

Life expectancy for an American born today is a little over 73 years. That means most of us will eventually spend some time in retirement, so it goes without saying that preparing for the years when we're not working has become an absolute necessity unless we want to face melted tuna casserole for dinner day in and day out during our golden years.

With very few exceptions, every American should have an IRA, Keogh, or *salary reduction plan*, or, if possible, all three. (A salary reduction plan is one in which your company deducts a certain percentage of your salary upon your request and puts it into a retirement account.) These may sound like stodgy ways to save, but the tax breaks offered by each of these three plans make saving very worthwhile; and fairly flexible rules provide a wide array of investment vehicles. In fact, few things in the financial world are as powerful and helpful as an IRA. According to investment advisers Scudder, Stevens, and Clark, if at age 25 you start to save $2,000 per year in an IRA yielding only 5 percent a year, you will accumulate $242,000 by age 65. At an annual rate of 10 percent that amount would grow to $885,000.

WHAT YOU WILL HAVE WHEN YOU ARE 65			
Age when start saving $2,000 per year in an IRA	Annual rate of return		
	5%	10%	15%
25	$242,000	$885,000	$3,558,000
35	133,000	329,000	869,000
45	66,000	115,000	205,000
55	25,000	32,000	41,000

An Individual Retirement Account

The Mechanics

What exactly is an IRA? It's an "individual retirement account" designed to help you save for the day when you or your spouse is no longer working. Legally, there is no official minimum for opening an IRA, but most plans require at least $250, and the benefits tend to be greater at that level: interest rates are higher, compounding is more generous, and there are more investment choices open to you with $250.

Anyone who is working can put up to 100 percent of the first $2,000 he or she earns annually into an IRA every year. If you earn less than $2,000 a year—let's say $1,275—you could contribute that entire amount. But even if you're a rock star making millions of dollars every year, $2,000 is still the maximum you can contribute annually.

Although there is a maximum yearly contribution, the account increases in value though the interest earned or the dividends paid out. These additional dollars stay in the account along with whatever you contribute, until you retire and begin withdrawing your money.

If both husband and wife are working, each can contribute $2,000 to separate accounts every year and take $4,000 off their joint income tax return. If one spouse does not work, then the working spouse can contribute up to $2,250. Note that in this

5

"spousal account," however, some portion of the money must be set aside in each spouse's name; it need not be equal amounts.

Whether you're inclined to be conservative or speculative, there's an investment program that's right for your retirement plan. The various choices are explained in this chapter.

First, let's look at some of the very convincing arguments for opening an IRA:

- There are generous tax benefits, both short term and long term, available to everyone who opens an IRA or Keogh Plan. Money put into an IRA can be deducted from your earnings before calculating your federal income tax, and returns earned in your IRA account are not taxed until they are withdrawn.

- The recent turmoil over the financial well-being of the Social Security system has, or should have, alerted everyone to the fact that it can no longer be counted on as basic income for retirement. Even government-supported medical benefits have been tightened, reducing the portion of a retiree's bill covered by the system. You should regard Social Security only as a means for covering subsistance-level items. At most, Social Security benefits replace only 28 percent of salary for someone earning $35,000 or more upon retirment.

- Companies are getting wise, too, and are not always inclined to be any more generous than they have to be. Pension plans are trending downward, and benefits are generally being reduced.

- Bailouts have been necessary to rescue the Social Security system, railroad, and other large federal retirement systems. And other private retirement systems consistently come under the gun as programs teeter under the weight of huge payments to beneficiaries. Keep in mind, too, that more and more companies are tapping pension coffers to raise dollars for expansion, mergers, etc. During the past several years, over 135 companies actually closed out their retirement plans. Many substituted less expensive programs. In some cases, disgruntled employees responded with law suits, charging that greedy CEOs (Chief Executive Officers) abused the retirement funds.

The winning aspect of an IRA, of course, is that the money you contribute is deductible from your taxable income. Interest earned in the account is *not* taxed until it is withdrawn—theoretically when you're retired and in a lower tax bracket.

But of course, there are strings attached to such a favorable plan:

- If you withdraw money before you are 59½ years old, it will hurt—you will be fined a 10 percent penalty above regular ordinary income tax.

- That's not the end. You must by law begin to withdraw money by the time you are 70½. Otherwise, there is a penalty.

If you don't have enough money to open an IRA, under certain circumstances it may actually make sense to borrow the money to do it with. Doesn't seem logical? It isn't unless you realize that while the interest earned on the money in your IRA is accumulating free of taxes, the interest you pay on the loan is tax deductible. So, if you're earning a higher rate of interest in the IRA (when the tax break is taken into consideration) than you are paying to borrow, it could be worth it to you. Your banker will help you determine if this is a wise move, given the interest and loan rates prevailing at the time.

Where

The safest and probably the most convenient choice for an IRA is a bank **CD** or Certificate of Deposit (See Chapter 10). It is insured up to $100,000, and rates are guaranteed for the entire investment period. In fact, the law requires sponsors of fixed-rate IRAs to tell you how much money you will have in your IRA before you reach retirement. Theoretically this allows you to compare various institutions (or "**custodians**," as they are officially called) and determine where you can get the most for your money.

Many banks, savings and loans, and credit unions charge little or nothing at all to set up and maintain an IRA. But don't count on it—some do indeed have monthly maintenance charges. That means, as in every institutional transaction, you must read the fine print carefully.

Banks offer IRA certificates of deposit that pay whatever rate the bank wants, and they vary considerably. Some have fixed yields; some even have variable yields that float up and down with general interest rates. Most banks require a $250 or $500 minimum to open a certificate of deposit for an IRA. Banks are not limited as to the time length of an IRA CD—they range from several months to several years, and money market accounts (see pp. 48–49) are also available. Remember: There's a risk involved in going long term, since rates may go up in the meantime, thus making your original investment with its locked-in interest rate less attractive. The shorter the time period, the more conservative your play. It is true you will lose some interest if rates fall, but the general thinking is that interest rates will probably stay the same or go up. If you lock in a long-term yield, you eliminate the chance of taking advantage of rising interest rates.

What if you have less than $250? It depends upon where you live, but in some banks you can still open an IRA for only $50; however, you will certainly get a lower interest rate, generally only 5½ percent. Do it anyway—then when you have accumulated enough money, you can transfer it into longer term, often without a fee.

The important points to keep in mind about a bank IRA are:

- The more money you have to invest, the greater number of options you will have to choose from.

- There are no government regulations limiting the type of IRA account banks can offer. Money market accounts and fixed-interest accounts are available as IRAs. The American Banking Association reports that most IRA money is in eighteen- or thirty-month certificates of deposit. Two-thirds of the customers selected fixed-rate CDs; the rest chose floating-rate certificates.

- Don't make the mistake of thinking that all banks and savings and loans offer the same deal. They don't. Terms vary widely and so do withdrawal and transfer penalties. Once again, it pays to get on the phone and find out who is offering what.

Other IRA Choices

Deciding where to put your IRA and Keogh dollars is very much related to personal temperament as well as market timing. If you tend to be cautious, or if you're nervous watching the stock market go up and down, then a bank CD as just described is probably your best bet. But if you enjoy playing the market and are astute in selecting stocks, consider putting your IRA with a broker.

Age, too, should play a role in your choice of custodian. Investors near retirement should be more conservative than those in their twenties. Fixed-income securities rather than speculative-growth stocks are a more logical choice.

Here is a thumbnail sketch of your custodian choices. Remember that although you can divide your IRA contributions into as many investment choices as you like (as long as you stay within the dollar limitations), it's best to keep those choices to a reasonable number. It's difficult to keep track of too many plans and to continually make that many investment decisions.

MUTUAL FUNDS. The inner workings of **mutual funds** are explained in great deatil in chapters 9, 11, and 14. But as far as the pros and cons of using one for you IRA or Keogh Plan are concerned, here is what you should know.

Just about all mutual funds—which are companies that pool money together from individuals in order to buy a wide variety of stocks, bonds, and nearly anything else—offer IRAs. Even though you can find a mutual fund specializing in gold or foreign stocks, your own good judgment should steer you in more sane directions. Remember—you're saving for your own retirement.

Look for mutual funds that invest in money market funds, common stocks selected for appreciation, and bonds aimed at high current income.

Avoid speculative stocks, commodities, hedge funds, gold and precious metals, and foreign funds. And steer clear of funds that are already tax exempt. Since IRAs are sheltered from taxes, you don't need that feature. Also, exempt funds tend to pay a slightly lower return than taxable funds.

How do mutual funds compare with bank CDs for your IRA or Keogh?

A MUTUAL FUND FOR YOUR IRA?

Pros	Cons
■ Potential for substantial gains	■ Not insured
■ For those prepared to take a calculated risk	■ Vulnerable to market risks
■ For those who don't want to pick their own stocks or bonds	■ Changes in value with the stock market or interest rates
■ Over the very long term, stocks tend to outpace other investments.	■ A fee is charged for setting one up
	■ There may be sale fees, too.
	■ Profits on stocks will be taxed at ordinary income tax rates. If you own stocks outside an IRA, capital gains are taxed at the more favorable rate of no more than 20 percent.

BROKERAGE HOUSES. At some point down the road, if you feel confident enough about picking stocks and you've been making maximum contributions to your IRA account for several years, you might consider opening a "self-directed" IRA through a brokerage firm. You will manage the funds, but the broker will serve as custodian, collecting the commission on your buy and sell trades.

When your IRA is small, this type of account hardly pays since you don't have enough funds with which to diversify. In other words, the amount is not sufficient to spread out over several different stocks or bonds. And, on top of that, the brokerage fees are high in relation to the size of your account. (See page 31 for a sample of commission fees.)

If eventually, however, you decide to run your own IRA, try doing it through a discount broker where the fees are substantially lower.

INSURANCE COMPANIES. You can buy an insurance annuity through most major life insurance companies. These provide a guaranteed monthly income for life. With a fixed annuity, the amount of your check never varies, even if inflation takes off. But the payout rate on a variable annuity does just that—it varies according to the yield of the investment or investments the annuity is based on.

Typically, insurance companies charge hefty fees for setting up an IRA annuity and for switching custodians, and they are generally not the ideal place for an IRA.

ZERO COUPON BONDS.* Because interest income is tax deferred in IRA and Keogh Plans, Treasury zero coupon bonds are well suited to these accounts. For example, a person planning to retire in 1998 might invest $179.37 and have at retirement $1,000. If he or she is able to invest $1,790, they will receive $10,000 in 1998.

Payoff of a Short-Term IRA

In both an IRA and Keogh Plan, eventually you reach what is called the "break even point" when you can take out funds, pay the nondeductible 10 percent penalty and taxes due, and still be ahead: that is, better off than if you had invested the same amount in a nonsheltered account. This chart shows how many years it takes to reach that point:

ANNUAL RETURN ON INVESTMENT

Tax Bracket	8%	10%	12%	15%
30%	7 yrs	6 yrs	5 yrs	4 yrs
35%	6½ yrs	5½ yrs	4½ yrs	4 yrs
40%	6½ yrs	5 yrs	4½ yrs	3½ yrs
45%	6 yrs	5 yrs	4½ yrs	3½ yrs
50%	6 yrs	5 yrs	4½ yrs	3½ yrs

* See Chapter 11 for a full explanation of how zero coupon bonds work to your advantage.

ADVANTAGES OF AN IRA

- Every dollar you contribute can be written off your tax return.

- An IRA is a way to set aside money for retirement.

- Contributions reduce your tax bill.

- Interest or dividends are tax free until withdrawn.

DISADVANTAGES OF AN IRA

- If you cash in your IRA early, you will face stiff penalties.

- IRAs are not liquid. Although you can withdraw money, the penalties for doing so are stiff.

- IRAs may not be used as collateral.

Banks, brokers, and mutual funds all have charts showing how much you will be ahead with an IRA. We have reproduced samples so you can study the benefits. Keep in mind that the inflation rate is not factored in on these charts, so the benefits are not quite as wonderful as they appear.

Investment performance in an IRA account far outstrips most similar investments made in the taxable world. This chart shows how long it takes an IRA investment to outpace a non-IRA investment. For example, someone in the 25 percent bracket whose investment earns 8 percent reaches the break-even point in the eighth year. If you're in the 50 percent bracket, it takes only six years.

ANNUAL YIELD ON YOUR INVESTMENT

Tax Bracket	8%	10%	12%	15%
25%	8 yrs	7 yrs	6 yrs	5 yrs
35%	7	6	5	4
50%	6	5	4	4

Helpful Hints

- If you're in the 44 percent tax bracket, putting $2,000 in an IRA has an after-tax cost of only $1,120 because the $2,000 deduction takes $880 off your income tax liability.

- If you and your spouse both work, you can write off $4,000 on a joint return even if your $2,000 each went into separate IRA accounts.

- When you reach 70½, you no longer can contribute to your IRA, but you can deposit up to $2,000 in a spousal account, if your spouse is under 70½ and doesn't work.

- If you're single with a taxable income of $35,000 and you put $2,000 in an IRA, your taxable income is reduced to $33,000. That will save you $717 in tax that would otherwise have to be paid. So, in effect, you are getting a $2,000 investment for $1,283.

- The law does not require that annual deposits be made all at once, so don't avoid an IRA just because you don't have $2,000 in one lump sum. Nor are you required to make deposits every year once you've started your account, although it's obviously to your advantage to do so.

- You can open a new account each year and split your contributions, channeling funds into different investment vehicles.

- You are allowed to change "custodians" as often as you like (A custodian is financial-eze for the institution that handles your IRA.) Simply tell the custodian where you want your money sent. There will probably to be a fee; if so this will be spelled out in the fine print of your IRA agreement.

- When should you *not* open an IRA? If you don't have the money and it's not feasible to borrow to finance the purchase of an IRA (see page 7), or if you know you'll need the cash before you are 59½.

You may have use of your IRA dollars once a year for a sixty-day period through a procedure called a **roll over** in which you actually take money out of one IRA account and put it into another one. But beware: Unless your assets are in another IRA within sixty days, you will have to pay both income tax and the added

10 percent penalty tax. Some people find a roll over useful if they need cash for less than sixty days.

Two of the most helpful booklets on IRAs are available for free. Contact your nearest office of the Internal Revenue Service for a copy of their Publication 590, *Individual Retirement Arrangements (IRA's)*.

For a copy of *Plan Tomorrow Today*, write to: Investment Company Institute, 1600 M Street N.W., Washington, DC 20036.

A Keogh Plan

If you are self-employed, either part-time or full-time, you should try to take advantage of the tax benefits offered by a Keogh Plan. Anyone who earns income from his or her own business, profession, or skill is entitled to participate in a Keogh as well as in an IRA.

Note: Even if you have an IRA or a private pension plan set up in which to save salaried income, you may still have a Keogh Plan in order to shelter that portion of your income that comes from being self-employed. If you are completely self-employed, however, you can still have both an IRA and a Keogh.

As with an IRA, you have a number of custodian choices: banks, savings and loans, brokerage houses, mutual funds, and insurance companies. And, as with the IRA, all your contributions are deductible from your federal income tax, and the interest in your account accumulates free of taxes. The same early withdrawal penalties apply as well.

Here's where the two plans differ: In a Keogh you may contribute up to 20 percent of what you earn through self-employment —before tax deductions—for a total of $30,000 annually. If you have high self-employed income, that's a much better deal than the $2,000 IRA maximum. On the other hand, if you're self-employed part-time, the 20 percent ceiling may be rather low.

PART TWO

Safe Stashing for Your First $50

3 The Institutional Cookie Jar

In your great-grandmother's day, the family savings were tucked away in a cookie jar, stuffed under the mattress, or hidden in a deep hole behind the back porch. People of your grandmother's generation, who lost money when many of the banks closed their doors in 1929, may still be putting their faith and their money in the land, just as Scarlett O'Hara's daddy advised.

Yet for most of us, the local bank still seems the most logical holding spot for that first $50. But not necessarily. Let's take a look at what your bank will do with your $50 and what other options you have.

Passbook and Statement Savings Bank Accounts

Not all banks are created equal, nor do all banks treat all customers equally. So, don't make a mad dash to the first bank on your corner. It pays to shop around, even with just $50 burning a hole in your pocket. Eventually you will become a larger depositor and will need to use the bank for other reasons—a loan, a mortgage, or a NOW or SuperNOW account. Some banks offer estate planning, courses in financial planning, and computerized investing—all services you may want later on.

Since most Americans are always in a hurry, the single most common factor in deciding where to bank is, of course, location. Yet, your nearest branch is not necessarily the right choice for you. Before opening a savings account, check out your neighborhood bank, by all means, but also make personal visits to several others. Don't worry about the quality of the wall-to-wall carpeting or the abundance of fresh flowers. Decor is, of course, not the issue. But other things certainly are:

Check to see:

- If all types of services are offered
- How well rush hour traffic is handled
- If there are express lines
- If there are branches near both where you live and where you work
- If there are bank officers accessible to answer questions, or if you are likely to be sent scurrying from one desk to another in a Kafkalike circle
- If there is written material available on interest rates and service charges

The last point is especially important when selecting a **commercial bank**, a **savings and loan association (S & L)**, or a **credit union** for your savings. Before we go any further, let's establish the differences among the three.

S & L's were originally called building and loan associations. Members pooled their savings so that they could borrow money to build houses. Today, S&Ls continue to specialize in home mortgages and often pay slightly higher interest on savings than commercial banks.

Commercial banks offer the widest range of services of all depository institutions. Initially they serviced only businesses, but starting in the early part of this century they began to solicit accounts from people from all walks of life. Today they offer every conceivable type of account, loan, and service.

Credit unions emerged in this country in the early 1900s to help those working class people who didn't qualify for loans from commercial banks. The members of a credit union pooled their money and made low-interest loans to one another. Today credit unions serve those with a common bond (see pages 24–27 for more on these institutions).

When you deposit $50 in a savings account at a commercial bank or S&L association, the maximum you will receive is 5½ percent—the top rate currently allowed by law. Credit unions pay as much as two to three percentage points higher.

The stated rate, however, is only the tip of the iceberg. It is also important to know exactly how often the interest will be paid, because every time your account is credited with interest, you will have that much more money to calculate on the next time interest is paid. In other words, the more frequently interest is compounded, the more money you will earn.

So, open your account at a bank where interest is compounded daily; it will provide a better return than if interest is compounded quarterly. In turn, quarterly is better than semiannually.

Despite the many and confusing ways in which bankers manage to figure interest on their savings accounts, your $50 is better off there than in the cookie jar because the temptation to put your hand in and spend it is greatly reduced—and, you will actually earn some interest.

The Passing of the Passbook

In many areas of the country, and especially in the larger cities, banks are phasing out or have already eliminated the traditional passbook savings account. In marches the **statement account** to take its place. Not good news for the small saver. Banks are obviously trying to eliminate the paperwork involved in maintaining passbook entry keeping. They much prefer statement accounts that issue a computerized update either monthly or quarterly. But the new deal is far less advantageous to the investor with only $50.

Whereas the old passbook savings account could be opened for as little as $15, the typical statement account usually has a higher minimum, often $100 to $500. In small towns, and in the South and Midwest, minimums tend to be lower than in the East and Northeast and in large cities. And in many banks, if your balance falls below a certain amount, you will lose interest, be assessed a monthly charge, or both.

For example, Citibank in New York requires a $500 minimum to open a statement savings account. Their interest rate is 5½ percent. If your balance falls below $500, a monthly fee of $1.50 is slapped on, so you could actually lose money because of the monthly charge. Citibank's passbook savings account can be opened for as little as $5. It has the same fee structure as the statement account, but it only pays 4½ percent.

You can see that it is no longer so easy to open a regular savings account for just $50 at a commercial bank.

On the other hand, savings and loan association banks are offering better deals for the small investor. The Dime Savings Bank in New York, like many others across the country, will open a savings account for only $5.00 and pay 5½ percent interest. But you could lose money here, too—the Dime charges $1.00 a month if your balance falls below $500.

Need we say more? Run a full information check on your bank!

Automatic Savings Plans

For those who spend every penny and always will, an **automatic savings plan** may be a solution. Similar to the **bank coupon clubs** (Christmas Clubs are a good example; we'll come to those in a minute), they operate through your local bank.

You decide how much you want to save—say, $50 a month—and then that amount is automatically transferred monthly from your checking account or from your paycheck into your savings account. The bank takes care of all the details. Sometimes a small service charge is attached to the plan.

As you develop your savings program and add to that first $50, eventually you will have several hundred dollars in the account. When you reach that point read Chapter 14 for suggestions about higher-yielding bank money market deposit accounts. By then, it's no longer prudent to leave your money in a savings account. Higher interest is beckoning just around the corner!

BANK SAVINGS ACCOUNT

For Whom
- Small saver
- Those with less than $500

Where to Open
- Bank
- Savings and loan association

Fee and Minimum Balance

- No opening fee
- Monthly fees vary if balance drops below certain level

Safety Factor

- High
- Deposits insured up to $100,000 at all FDIC (Federal Deposit Insurance Corporation) -insured institutions.

Advantages

- Safety
- Geographically accessible
- Withdrawal upon demand
- Principal is guaranteed up to $100,000 by federally backed insurance corporation if bank is FDIC insured.

Disadvantages

- Interest rate is low and fixed.
- Checks cannot be written.
- Monthly fees on low balances may mean you will lose money.

Coupon Clubs

It's certainly gimmicky, but if it helps you save, then give the bank coupon club a try.

The coupon club is the generic name for a myriad of programs devised by banks to attract business. These include Christmas clubs, Hanukkah clubs, vacation clubs, and so forth. Also offered by savings and loan associations and credit unions, they are especially popular with those who like tearing coupons out of books.

If you decide to join one, each week or month, depending upon the club, you will make a specified deposit or payment, enclosing a coupon with your money. At the end of a stated period, usually a year, your coupons will all be gone and your account full of money. In some clubs you cannot withdraw your money until the stated period is over.

Couponless Plans

In some banks, you can sign up for automatic savings deposits plans if you make the arrangements. You designate the monthly amount you want to save, let's say $35. This amount is then automatically taken out of your checking account and deposited into your savings account. Interest rates, which are fixed, vary—5 to 6 percent is standard. The record of your transaction is then attached to your regular checking account statement.

COUPON CLUBS

For Whom

- Undisciplined savers
- People with large families who have to buy lots of holiday gifts
- Those who like tearing along perforated lines

Fee

- Usually none

Safety

- High

Advantages

- Forced way to save

Disadvantages

- Some clubs pay low interest or not interest at all.
- Some pay interest only if you complete the full term of the club.
- You may not be able to withdraw your money until the full year is over.

A Bank Checkup

- Ask your banker how interest is compounded.

- Get a printed chart of interest rates to study at home.

- Ask if the bank pays interest only on the lowest balance during the quarter. For example, if you have $200 in your account and you take out $75, then eventually build it back up to $200, is interest paid as though you had had only $125 in the account all the time?

- Look for a bank paying interest from day of deposit to day of withdrawal.

- Will you be charged extra if you make many withdrawals?

- Are there any days at the end of the quarter when interest is not paid?

- How many days are in the bank's year? (Some banks have "dead days" at the end of a quarter when they don't pay interest.)

- If you take out money, or close the account at mid-quarter, will you lose interest?

- Are there penalties for leaving your account inactive for a long period?

Study carefully the chart on annually compounded interest in a $50 account and use it as a guideline for making your banking decision.

$50 COMPOUNDED AT 5½ PERCENT

	In 1 Year	In 5 Years	In 10 Years	In 20 Years
Daily	$53.73	$71.66	$102.71	$211.00
Monthly	52.82	65.85	86.73	150.43
Quarterly	52.81	65.77	86.51	149.68
Semiannually	52.79	65.58	86.02	147.99
Annually	52.75	65.35	85.41	145.89

How Safe Is Your Bank?

In 1983, the Federal Deposit Insurance Corporation revealed that nearly 600 banks were on their "problem list"—which meant that some of them could become insolvent, or even fail.

Don't take a chance. Put your account in a bank that has FDIC insurance, in which case you will be insured for up to $100,000 by the FDIC. Of the 15,447 commercial banks in the U.S., most (14,776) have this insurance. Just make certain your money is not in one of the 666 that doesn't. The FDIC is an independent agency of the U.S. Government established by Congress in 1933 to insure bank deposits. The bank pays for the cost of insurance through semiannual assessments based on its volume of deposits. For an explanation of what FDIC insurance does and does not do, write to the FDIC (550 17th Street N.W., Washington, DC 20429) for a free copy of *Your Insured Deposit*.

Credit Unions

Once thought of only as a place for assembly line workers to get a car loan, **credit unions** have taken on a brand new look. They are a viable choice for your $50, and they usually pay two to three percentage points above the top commercial savings rate, which is 5½ percent. There is no lid on interest rates; they vary from union to union.

Credit unions are cooperatives, or not-for-profit associations of people who pool their savings and then lend money to one another. By law, they must have so-called "common bonds," which may consist in working for the same employer, belonging to the same church, club, or government agency, or even living in the same neighborhood. Because they are not-for-profit and because overhead costs are low, credit unions almost always give savers and borrowers better rates and terms than commercial institutions.

There are more than 20,000 U.S. credit unions with assets in excess of $90 billion. While the largest, the Navy Federal Credit Union, has 580,000-plus members, the average has 2,200.

Today's upbeat union bears very little resemblance to the cooperatives established some seventy-five years ago in order to save working-class people from the ubiquitous loan shark. These feisty cooperatives have aggressively expanded their turf, offering a line of sophisticated financial services and often competing very favorably with commercial banks and savings and loans. Many, in fact, operate like local banks.

Theoretically, unions are run by the depositors—every member, in fact, must be a depositor, albeit a very small one, although the true organizational work is done by volunteer committees in the smaller unions and by paid employees in the larger groups.

If you are not already a member of a credit union, but would like to be one, write to the industry's trade organization for a list of the unions you might be able to join:

Credit Union National Association
P.O. Box 431
Madison, WI 53701

But before you invest your $50 in a credit union:

- Make sure the union is insured either by a federal agency or the National Credit Union Administration.

- Inquire about its reputation from members.

If you are interested in starting a credit union, contact the CUNA, or the nearest regional office of the National Credit Union Administration. This group supervises and insures federal credit unions.

NATIONAL CREDIT UNION ADMINISTRATION
REGIONAL OFFICES

Address	Area Served
Region I (Boston) 441 Stuart Street, 6th Floor Boston, MA 02116 Telephone 617-223-6807	Connecticut, Maine, Massachusetts, New Hampshire, New Jersey, New York, Puerto Rico, Rhode Island, Vermont, Virgin Islands
Region II (Capital) 1776 G Street N.W. Suite 700 Washington, DC 20006 Telephone 202-682-1900	Delaware, District of Columbia, Maryland, Pennsylvania, Virginia, West Virginia
Region III (Atlanta) 1365 Peachtree Street N.E. Suite 500 Atlanta, GA 30367 Telephone 404-881-3127	Alabama, Arkansas, Florida, Georgia, Kentucky, Louisiana, Mississippi, North Carolina, South Carolina, Tennessee

Region IV (Chicago)

230 South Dearborn
Suite 3346
Chicago, IL 60604
Telephone 312-886-9697

Illinois, Indiana, Iowa,
Michigan, Minnesota,
Missouri, North Dakota,
Ohio, South Dakota,
Wisconsin

Region V (Austin)

611 East 6th Street
Suite 407
Telephone 512-482-5131

Denver Sub Office-
  Lea Complex
10455 East 25th Avenue
Aurora, CO 80010
Telephone 303-837-3795

Arizona, Colorado, Idaho,
Kansas, Montana, Nebraska,
Nevada, New Mexico,
Oklahoma, Texas, Utah,
Wyoming

Region VI (San Francisco)

77 Geary Street, 2nd Floor
San Francisco, CA 94108
Telephone 415-556-6277

Alaska, American Samoa,
California, Guam, Hawaii,
Oregon, Washington

For Whom

- Members and members' families

Where to Find

- Your place of work
- Your neighborhood association
- Church, club, synagogue
- Sources listed on pages 25–26

Minimum

- You must buy at least one share to join a credit union.
- Shares are determined by each union and vary from $5 to $30, with most around $15. (A share is really your first deposit.)

Safety

- Varies, but generally above average

Advantages

- Interest rates on savings are generally higher than at commercial institutions.
- Interest rates on loans are generally lower than at commercial institutions.
- Other services may be offered, such as mortgages, credit cards, NOW-type accounts (see pages 39–42), IRAs.
- An automatic payroll deduction savings plan is frequently available.
- Purchase of stocks listed on the New York Stock Exchange and other exchanges is possible at low commissions.

Disadvantages

- Might be run by inexperienced volunteers
- Might be inadequately staffed
- Might not be adequately insured

5 Turning to Uncle Sam

The bank isn't the only safe slow-growth investment vehicle for your $50. Uncle Sam is willing and eager to keep it for you and, in return, provide a little something in the way of interest through what is known as a **U.S. Savings Bond**. When you buy a U.S. Savings Bond you are lending money to the U.S. Goverment.

A few years ago, the government savings bond program was known as the dog of the investment world. It played upon the heartstrings of all good Americans, using the theme of patriotism to lure in the money. Often, low-income families sank all they had into savings bonds only to end up earning interest well below average. When inflation, for instance, was at 10 percent, the government was paying a measly 6.5 percent—hardly something the Treasury officials could have been proud of.

Since then, the program has been revamped, revised, and remarketed. Now the Series EE Savings Bonds are a viable way to save small amounts of money (known as preserving capital) and at the same time earn interest.

You can buy EE bonds at your bank in multiples of $25. The purchase price is actually 50 percent of the bond's face value, so in other words, a $50 bond costs only $25.* Series EE bonds mature in ten years plus two months, so if you hold your bond to maturity, you will double your money—that is, you'll get back the face value, $50 per bond in the case of a $25 bond, plus variable interest. In addition to buying these bonds at the bank, you may also buy them through automatic payroll deductions, as thousands of employers participate in the savings bond program. This is a good way to save if you're not a natural saver. In fact, after a while you may not even miss the $25 from your paycheck.

---

*EE Savings Bonds are sold in the following face value amounts: $50, $75, $100, $200, $500, $1,000, $5,000, and $10,000.

28

These bonds pay 4.16 percent for the first six months and 5.5 percent for the first year. Then, the yield rises 25 percent every six months up to five years. After five years, you will earn interest equal to 85 percent of the average yield paid on five-year **Treasury notes** (see page 74). If for some reason the five-year Treasury note yield drops below 7.5 percent, you're in luck because the government guarantees a minimum of 7.5 percent on all EE bonds held for five years or more. In other words, these bonds pay whichever rate is higher.

Let's say the average Treasury note rate is 11 percent. You would earn 85 percent of that, or 9.35 percent. But if it were only 6.5 percent, you would still receive 7.5 percent.

If you redeem your bond between six months and five years after purchase, you will get back your full investment, that is $25 per bond, plus the earned interest.

If you cash in your bond before five years are up you won't earn the top rate of interest. Here's the current schedule:

- Between six months and a year, the rate is 5.5%.

- Between one and two years, the rate is   6.0%.

- Between two and three years, the rate is   6.5%.

- Between three and four years, the rate is   7.0%.

- Between four and five years, the rate is   7.5%

You cannot, however, redeem your bond *at all* during the first six months.

EE SAVINGS BONDS

For Whom

- Those who won't need the money until five years have passed

- Those who want a competitive deferred yield

- Those who have a low tolerance for risk and want to be certain that their principal is safe

Where to Purchase

- Banks

- Payroll savings plan

- Savings and loan associations
- Credit unions
- Federal Reserve Bank (see addresses on page 79–80)
- Bureau of the Public Debt, Securities Transaction Branch, Washington, DC 20226

Fee and Minimum

- No fee
- Minimum purchase, $25 for a $50 bond

Safety Rating

- Highest possible

Advantages

- Virtually no risk because the principal is government-backed and interest is default proof
- Can be cashed in at full purchase value ($25 each) before redemption date of five years
- In fact, if you buy a bond in your child's name, he or she might get the interest totally tax free. You can set up an automatic eduction fund by purchasing bonds in your child's name and timing the purchase so the bonds come due when your child goes to college. The advantage of doing this is that your child is in a much lower tax bracket than you are. There is no tax if the child's investment and other unearned income is under $1,000 per year. Between $1,000 and $6,000 a year the tax rate varies from 12 percent to 16 percent.
- Upon maturity, you may reinvest, or roll over, your Series EE Savings Bonds into Series HH bonds and further defer your taxes until the HH bonds mature, another ten years down the road. HH bonds can only be purchased by rolling over EE bonds that have reached maturity and are available in denominations of $500.

6 Mini-Investor Programs

Once you have tucked away a small nest egg, then $50, believe it or not, can move you into the stock market. There are several interesting programs especially designed for the mini-investor; but remember, stocks are more risky than any of the previously mentioned vehicles. These mini-programs are not designed to take the place of a savings account. They are merely an inexpensive way to buy stocks. Participation is suggested only after you have saved up in other ways for an emergency.

Unfortunately, many brokers who once welcomed small investors discourage them today by charging high commissions on small trades. For example, 100 shares of a $50 stock will cost between $90 and $98 in brokerage commissions from "full-service" firms like Merrill Lynch, E. F. Hutton, Paine Webber, and so forth. A discount firm, on the other hand, charges between $30 and $50 for the same purchase. (Full details about buying stocks can be found in Chapter 17.)

Yet, there are several ways you can get into the action with your $50 and at a reasonable rate.

Buying Stock Directly

You can bypass stockbrokers altogether by going directly to the company. Only a handful of public companies offer this unique service, but you can expect more to join the bandwagon. They include:

W. R. Grace & Company
Shareholder Relations Department
1114 Avenue of the Americas
New York, NY 10036

Control Data Corporation
Stockholder Services HQNOII
8100 34 Avenue South
Bloomington, MN 55420

Barnett Banks of Florida*
Customer Stock Purchase Plan
P.O. Box 2507
Jacksonville, FL 32231

You can purchase stock directly from the company, if you live in an area serviced by the following utility companies:

Carolina Power & Light
Central Hudson Gas & Electric
Central Maine Power
Cleveland Electric Illuminating
Dominion Resources
Duke Power

Idaho Power
Montana Power
Portland General Electric
Puget Sound Power & Light
San Diego Gas & Electric
Union Electric

Hint: If there is a company you're interested in, you can inquire by writing to them directly. Address your letter to the Shareholder Relations Department.

Even if you only own one share in a company, sometimes you can participate in the **dividend reinvestment plan (DRP)** which permits shareholders to buy additional stock by automatically reinvesting dividends.

You can get a list of over 700 firms offering DRPs by sending $2 to:

Standard & Poor's Corporation
Public Relations Department
25 Broadway
New York, NY 10004

You must have an account at this bank in order to buy shares directly.

Another list of selected companies with DRPs is available for $1 from:

> United Business Service
> Attention: Stanley Rice
> 210 Newbury Street
> Boston, MA 02116

(For more information on DRPs, see Chapter 17.)

Low-Cost Ways
To Buy Stocks

As an individual, it is possible to join the National Association of Investment Clubs, NAIC (address and more information on page 37); as a member you can purchase one share of any stock from a selected group of companies, and NAIC will handle your investment.

To cover the handling costs, the NAIC has a one-time charge of $5 for each stock you buy.

An increasing number of companies offer plans through which employees can buy stock in the company. Check with your personnel division to see if your employer offers this option. According to the Employees Benefit Research Institute, the most popular plan is one that permits employees to contribute up to 6 percent of their salary and then the firm matches half that contribution.

The Sharebuilder Plan

An inexpensive and convenient way for you to invest in stocks has been devised by Merrill Lynch, the nation's largest full-service brokerage firm. Through the **Sharebuilder Plan**, you can now invest any dollar amount you want, the minimum being $25. The interesting aspect of this program is that you're investing by the dollar amount, *not* by the share, which means you can acquire fractions of shares as well as whole units. You may select the companies you want to invest in, or you can use Merrill Lynch's list of recommended stocks for participants in the Sharebuilder Plan. This list, updated periodically, will be sent to participants upon request. It consists of stocks with above-average dividend yields or long-term growth potential.

The Sharebuilder participants get a break on commissions. The firm charges up to 40 percent less than regular Merrill Lynch fees on transactions under $5,000.

SHAREBUILDER PLAN

For Whom

- Any small investor interested in getting into the market with minimal expenditures

Where to Purchase

- Your local Merrill Lynch office, or from:
  Sharebuilder
  P.O. Box 520
  Church Street Station
  New York, NY 10008

Minimum and fees

- $25
- Commission is discounted by 40% from regular fees.

Safety Factor

- Like any stock purchase, safety depends upon the price changes in the stock.

Advantages

- Low entry cost
- Merrill Lynch research and professional assistance
- Diversification
- Liquidity
- Reduced brokerage fees
- Optional automatic dividend reinvestment plan
- If you choose to have Merrill Lynch hold your certificates, they will be insured against loss up to $500,000.
- Company annual report will be sent to you as soon as you have one full share of any security.
- Record keeping and tax data are taken care of by Merrill Lynch.

Disadvantages

- Risk is equal to that of the stock market.

Baby Bonds

Traditionally, corporate or private bonds (as opposed to U.S. Government bonds) have been sold in denominations of $1,000 (see pages 57–63). But, beginning in 1984, a few companies and brokerage firms began to imitate the government's small-denomination Series EE Savings Bonds by issuing what Wall Street calls **baby bonds** for only $25.

The first to appear were issued by the DiGiorgio Corporation, a food-processing and distribution company. Merrill Lynch and Dean Witter handled 800,000 of these bonds, which sold for $25 each.

Merrill Lynch is now periodically offering **convertible** baby bonds that can later be changed, or converted, into stock at a price higher than the market value of the stock at the time the bond was sold.

Check with your broker or nearest Merrill Lynch office for the most recent material on these small-denomination corporate bonds.

35

7 Investment Clubs

O f all the options you have at your doorstep, a clubhouse will provide you with the most fun and enjoyment—if not the greatest return on your principal—as a home for your $50.

Joining an investment club is an excellent way to learn about the stock market, the movement of interest rates, and the overall economy. It is also a great way to meet new people who, like you, are interested in learning how to handle a small amount of money.

Most clubs are small—optimum size is about twenty—and they meet once or twice a month in a community center or in a member's home. Members pool their money and jointly purchase shares of stock. Clubs require monthly payments which can range from $20 per month to as high as the members dare go. Energetic hosts frequently combine the regular business meeting and discussion with coffee, dessert, or other refreshments.

The mechanics are simple. Making money, though, is not— especially if most members are inexperienced. Nevertheless, you will get your investment feet wet, and by combining your collective dollars and knowledge, who knows—you might pick a winner or two!

When putting togther an investment club, you might keep in mind that co-ed clubs seem to do best. A recent National Association of Investment Clubs study revealed that women's clubs are averaging 29 percent annual earnings compared with 21.7 percent for all-male clubs. Best of all are the mixed clubs, which are reporting 32.4 percent in earnings.

If you don't know of a club in your area, ask at work or at a local YMCA or YWCA, adult education center, church, or synagogue. If you cannot find a club to join, start your own with a few friends or colleagues. The steps are easy:

1. Find twelve to twenty people willing to join a club. Set the mini-

mum investment requirement ahead of time—$25 per month is common.

2. Select a person to be responsible for paper work. This task should rotate every few months.

3. Write to the National Association of Investment Clubs, 1515 East Eleven Mile Road, Royal Oak, Michigan 48067, for details on how to get started. Your club may join this association for $25, plus $4.50 per member. You will receive a stack of useful literature plus a subscription to *Better Investing* magazine. The NAIC also gives advice on organizing, conducting meetings, analyzing stocks, and setting up portfolios.

4. Establish firm guidelines regarding withdrawal of a member's funds and entry of new members.

5. Meet and invest on a regular basis—whether or not the market is doing well.

6. Reinvest all earnings in a diversified portfolio—one that has at least five different companies.

7. Use a discount broker to save on commission fees.

8. Stick to regular stock buy-and-sell procedures. All members should be responsible, on a regular, rotating basis, for doing research and making recommendations to the club.

INVESTMENT CLUBS

For Whom

- Anyone

Minimum

- Set by individual clubs. Ranges from $20 per month up. Members contribute the set amount on a monthly basis.

Safety Factor

- Probably slightly below average; depends on club.

Advantages

- Inexpensive and supportive way to learn about investing

- Reduces anxiety surrounding first-time investing and selling
- Individual members of the NAIC can buy one share of any of a number of companies and thereafter invest as little as $25 periodically (see page 33).

Disadvantages

- You could earn a better return elsewhere, especially if your club is inexperienced.
- Results are not guaranteed.
- Investment is not insured.
- High mortality rate—many clubs fail in the first twelve to eighteen months.

HOW YOUR $50 WILL GROW	One Year	Five Years	Ten Years
Commercial Savings Bank (5¼% compounded daily)	$52.63	$54.86	$ 71.67
S & L Association (5.5% compounded daily)	53.73	71.66	102.71
EE Savings Bond (7.5% compounded semiannually)	53.82	72.82	104.41
Coupon Club (6% compounded monthly)	53.08	67.44	90.97

PART THREE

The
First $500

8 The How &
Why of a NOW

Until recently, the advantage of having cash—that is, money in your pocket or in your savings account—was that it provided a reserve and was there, available immediately, whenever you needed it. But you probably never harbored any wild notions that you would make a lot of money with your idle cash, just a little interest from the bank. But in the last decade or so interest rates have risen to undreamed-of heights. Rates paid to the average investor on cash balances have climbed from 5 to 15 percent at times.

Therefore, holding cash itself has turned into an investment choice and has taken on new meaning within the financial world.

In response to the recent rise in interest rates and the subsequent deregulation of banks, there are now a number of investment choices for holding cash:

- NOW and SuperNOW bank accounts
- Treasury notes of two years or less

- Money Market mutual funds

- Insured Money Market bank accounts

- Bank certificates of deposit (CDs) of two years or less

For the moment, let's take a look at **NOW accounts**. NOW stands for Negotiable Order of Withdrawal, and basically a NOW account is an interest-bearing checking account. It's like a regular checking account with printed checks and regular statements, but it *also* pays interest—5¼ percent generally. Basically, a NOW account is a handy housekeeping account that permits you to earn a little interest on your cash balance as you pay bills.

NOWs have not always been around—that's why December 31, 1980, was a landmark day for American savers. That was the day federally regulated banks and savings and loan associations were permitted to offer NOW accounts to the eager public. Sounds good. But there are several caveats attached. In order to earn the 5¼ percent, a minimum or monthly average balance must be maintained. These minimums vary nationwide from about $300 to several thousand dollars.

If you fall below the required minimum balance, you will lose interest and you may also be subject to per-check, per-deposit, and/or monthly charges.

The equivalent of the NOW account at a credit union is called a **share draft**. Since credit unions do not have a cap on the amount of interest they can pay, share drafts generally offer slightly higher rates than bank NOW accounts.

Before opening a NOW account, quiz your banker and get precise answers to these questions:

- How is the minimum balance determined? Most banks add up your balance at the end of each day. If you're short, even for one day, you're slapped with a full service fee.

- If you fall below the minimum, what will you be charged? Banks have devised several clever ways of addressing this question. Some charge you for every check written during the month; others only for those written during the time when you were below minimum requirements. Another variation on the theme: You'll be charged only if you write more than a certain number of checks, say fifteen or twenty. Regardless of the methods used by the bank, it only pays to have a NOW account *if* you keep up the balance.

- How is the interest figured? Again, as in a passbook savings account, (see pages 16–18) you will get the best deal if your interest is figured from day of deposit to day of withdrawl, or on your daily average balance.

In the competitive banking world of today, a NOW account is a good choice *if* you can maintain the minimum amount in order to avoid having to pay steep fees and charges that eat up any earned interest. But do your calculations carefully. If you know maintaining the balance will be difficult, you will be better off with a regular checking account.

NOW CHECKING ACCOUNT

For Whom

- Ideal for anyone who wants a checking account and can maintain the bank's minimum balance at all times.

Minimum

- Varies from around $300 to $3,000 or more

Safety Factor

- Insured up to $100,000

Advantages

- You can earn interest on a checking account.

- You can write an unlimited number of checks of any amount.

Disadvantages

- Bank charges on regular checking accounts are almost universally lower than on NOW accounts.

- Minimums for maintaining NOW accounts are steep.

- Regular checking accounts sometimes toss in a few free extras, such as no charge for checks, toasters, and so forth. NOWs don't.

After you have taken care of opening your checking account —either the regular variety or a NOW account—the next $500 you accumulate should be transferred to one of the higher-paying parking places where you can earn almost twice as much interest as in a NOW or passbook savings account.

First we will examine the pros and cons of the money market mutual fund and then we will move on to Treasury notes and bonds, CDs, and SuperNOW accounts.

9 Money Market Mutual Funds

After you've established your IRA and opened a checking account, then saved $500, the next step is to find a safe place to put your hard-earned savings. One choice is a **money market mutual fund** where you can earn almost twice as much as in a regular savings account or a NOW checking account. A money market mutual fund is really just a special kind of mutual fund—which, in turn, is an investment company. When you participate in a mutual fund you are buying shares in an investment trust or corporation. This means that your investment dollars are pooled with those of hundreds of other investors and the combined total is invested by a professional manager in various investment vehicles. The fund manager studies the market, interest rates, and other economic indicators, buying and selling those investments that best suit the fund's stated aims or goals.

There's Power in Numbers

The value of a fund is that one large pool of money can be far more effectively invested than hundreds or thousands of small sums. Each investor, no matter how large or small his investment, then owns a proportional share of the fund, and receives a proportional return, without discrimination based on the number of shares owned.

Each fund has differing objectives. Some are set up for long-term growth, some for immediate income, others for tax-free returns. Some are willing to take higher levels of risk than others. Some are devoted exclusively to buying and selling stocks; others to bonds, or a combination of the two.

In the case of a money market mutual fund, the goal is a maximum return with minimum risk. Money market funds derive their name from the type of securities they invest in—"money market" securities.

Financial companies, large corporations, and the U.S. Government all borrow large sums of money for short priods (one year or less) by issuing **money market securities** in exchange for cash. For example, the government borrows by way of Treasury bills (T-bills) and notes; large corporations by IOUs called commercial paper; and banks by way of large certificates of deposit called CDs.

These money market securities make up the fund's portfolio, rather than stocks and bonds.

The borrowers—the government, large corporations, and banks—are good risks. They consist of the country's most solid institutions, and they all agree to pay back the money quickly and at high rates. That's why today you can earn almost double the traditional passbook savings account rate.

Obviously no ordinary saver would be able to participate in this venture on his or her own. The amounts involved are too large. But through a money market mutual fund, many average investors can share in this opportunity at relatively minimal cost.

So, by pooling your money with other investors and purchasing these T-bills, CDs, and other money market securities, you can lend to large institutions and gain high yields because the money earned by the fund, after expenses, is in turn paid out to you, the shareholder, as interest or "dividends."

Most funds require a minimum deposit of $1,000 and insist that additional deposits be at least $100.

A key point in favor of these funds is their liquidity. You have almost immediate access to your money without penalty. You can cash in your shares either by phone, by mail, or through your broker. Frequently, in fact, you can have money wired from the fund directly to your local bank.

In most funds, you can also tap the money by writing checks against your shares. Generally a fund permits unlimited check writing as long as the checks are for amounts over $500.

Two funds, however, will accept checks with a minimum of $250.

John Hancock Cash Management Trust
617-421-2910

Money Market Management
800-245-2423—outside Pennsylvania
412-228-1948—in Pennsylvania

There are more than 300 of these money market mutual funds open to individual savers. For a complete free list of money market funds, write to:

The Investment Company Institute
1600 M Street N.W.
Washington, DC 20036
202-293-7700

This pamphlet contains the names, addresses, and toll-free telephone numbers as well a the initial and subsequent investment minimums of each fund.

You may also find it helpful to read the brochure entitled "A Beginner's Guide to Money Funds," which is available free from:

Money Fund Safety Ratings
3471 North Federal Highway
Fort Lauderdale, FL 33306
305-563-9000

If you have less than $1,000 to invest, you can still participate in a money fund. Two funds have no minimum

Cash & Plus Trust
800-345-1151

First Trust Money Market Mutual Fund
800-621-4770

Several funds have only $500 minimums for opening:

American Shares
800-237-0738

Daily Cash Accumulation
800-525-9310

Franklin Group Money Funds
800-227-6781—outside California
800-632-2180—in California

AARP U.S. Government Money Market Trust*
800-245-4770—outside Pennsylvania
412-392-6300—in Pennsylvania

After digesting the material in the two pamphlets, take time to check the current yields of the funds in the newspaper. Pick out several funds, then call or write away for a copy of each fund's prospectus. This will tell you what instruments are in the fund's portfolio as well as give an indication of its past performance. If you're still uncertain about which fund to invest in, talk with your accountant or broker.

In selecting a fund, ask yourself these questions:

- What minimum investment can I afford?

- Do I want a fund nearby, through my broker, or can I invest by telephone or by wire?

- How easily can I redeem my shares? What is the fund's policy about writing checks? Will the fund wire money to my bank? How long will it take?

- Can I transfer from this fund to another if the economic climate changes? (See Family of Funds, page 87–90)

- What types of securities does the fund invest in? Would I feel safe in a different type of fund, say one that invests only in government securities?

Open only to members of the American Association for Retired Persons.

Safety

How safe are money market funds? Although they are not federally insured, in the course of the twelve years of their existence, only one money market fund has ever failed: First Multifund of New York, which was paying an extremely high rate —93 cents on the dollar—back in 1979.

If you are very concerned with safety, you should select a fund that has a high portion of U.S. Government securities in its portfolio, as well as CDs from well known domestic banks and top-rated commercial paper (i.e., IBM, General Electric, Exxon, etc.). You can find out about what is offered by writing or calling the fund and asking for a copy of the prospectus which lists its investments.

The safest funds of all, of course, are those that invest *only* in U.S. guaranteed securities. You will, of course, sacrifice a point or two in exchange for safety. For a free list of these, with their addresses and telephone numbers, write to:

Donoghue's Money Letter
P.O. Box 411
Holliston, MA 01746
617-429-5930

Among the better known funds that invest exclusively in U.S. guaranteed securities are:

Capital Preservation Fund
755 Page Mill Road
Palo Alto, CA 94304
800-227-8380

Merrill Lynch Government Fund
125 High Street
Boston, MA 02110
800-225-1576

Fidelity U.S. Government Reserves
Fidelity Investments
82 Devonshire Street
Boston, MA 02109
800-225-6190

Government Investors Trust
1655 North Fort Myer Drive
Arlington, VA 22209
800-336-3063

Vanguard Money Market Trust Federal Portfolio
P.O. Box 2600
Valley Forge, PA 19482
800-523-7025

Financial Planners Federal Securities
1730 K Street N.W.
Washington, DC 20006
800-424-8570
800-223-1000

Midwest Income Trust/Short Term Government Fund
Midwest Group of Funds
c/o MGF Service Corporation
Box 85354
Cincinnati, OH 45201
800-543-0407

Incidentally, don't pick a fund just because it has the word "government" in its name. That doesn't guarantee safety! Rather, it means that the odds are that the fund invests primarily in government securities. Unfortunately, however, not all funds are scrupulous about the meaning their name implies.

Another method for ensuring low risk is to select a fund with holdings of less than fifty days. In other words, if a fund's capital is invested in longer-term holdings and then if interest rates rise significantly, that fund's yield to you will be lower than those of funds holding shorter-term issues. In that event, a large number of fund owners might want to sell their shares in order to move into a higher-paying fund. In an extreme case—and it would indeed be extreme—the fund might be forced to sell assets at a loss.

Actually, money market mutual funds *are* quite safe. *They invest only in very short-term securities*, which helps them to maintain their liquidity and to insulate themselves from negative interest-rate movement. These securities usually mature in less than two months. And, by law, only 5 percent of a fund's assets may be held in obligations of any one institution other than obligations of the

U.S. Government. This ruling further adds to the safety of the funds.

Among the funds that are known for their safety are:

Kemper Money Market Fund
120 South LaSalle Street
Chicago, IL 60603
312-781-1121
800-621-0322

Dreyfus Liquid Assets
767 Fifth Avenue
New York, NY 10153
800-645-6561
212-895-1206

The dividends you earn on most funds are fully taxable. Some funds, however, invest solely in tax-exempt securities. Therefore their dividends are not taxed by the IRS, only by the state and local government.

A note of caution: Unless you are in a high tax bracket, it doesn't pay to buy into a tax exempt fund (see chart, page 51). These funds have *very* low yields and generally pay about half the rate of regular funds.

For the day when your taxable income hits $50,000, you may want to investigate:

Dreyfus Tax-Exempt Money Market Fund
800-645-6561—outside New York
212-895-1206—in New York

Franklin Tax-Free Income Fund
800-227-6781—outside California
800-632-2180—in California

Lexington Tax-Free Daily Income Fund
800-526-4791

Vanguard Municipal Bond Fund Money Market Portfolio
800-523-7025—outside Pennsylvania
800-362-0530—in Pennsylvania

Toasters and Teddy Bears

A number of money market funds are expanding their services, in an effort to keep your money and prevent you from being tempted to shift over to a bank or S&L's money market account (for more on those money markets, see page 8). Here are the names of several funds that have "extra goodies":

The Reserve Fund joined with Pittsburgh's Mellon Bank and is offering a cash-mangement fund for those customers who have $10,000 or more. You get unlimited checking on your Reserve Fund account, a Visa and MasterCard, a $2,000 unsecured line of credit, and monthly consolidated statements of all transactions plus a year-end tax summary.

The Vanguard Group has started a privately insured money market fund. St. Paul Fire and Marine Company will guarantee against any default in the fund's investments. Individual accounts will be covered up to $2 million each.

The Dreyfus Corporation purchased a bank in East Orange, New Jersey, which it subsequently renamed Dreyfus Consumer Bank. It has low-rate loans for those New Jersey residents who own shares in any of the Dreyfus funds, undercutting those offered by commercial banks, because most of their business is done by mail—which is less expensive than doing business in person.

Several services provide continually updated professional rankings and safety ratings of the money market mutual funds. Call or write for complimentary copies of the following newsletters:

"Money Fund Safety Ratings" (monthly; $49/year)
Institute for Econometric Research
3471 North Federal Highway
Fort Lauderdale, FL 33306
305-563-9000

"American Money Reporter" (every two weeks;
Marpep Publishing Ltd. $95 per year)
13 River Street
Sidney, NY 13838
212-758-2280

"Donoghue's Money Letter" (twice monthly; $87/year
P.O. Box 411   includes two semiannual
Holliston, MA 01746   directories)
617-429-5930

Two funds allow you to write checks for any amount—which essentially means your money fund turns into a checking account paying top interest rates:

Reserve CPA Account 800-223-5547

- Costs $50 per year, which includes a Visa and MasterCard
- No other service charge, no matter how many checks you write

Liquid Green Trust 800-862-7283

- No annual fee
- 30¢ per check if it is for less than $300
- If you are tied in with the firm's discount brokerage service, there is no charge for checks below $300

WHAT KINDS OF THINGS MONEY MARKET FUNDS BUY

Agency securities. Issued by government agencies such as Government National Mortgage Association (Ginnie Mae) and the Small Business Administration or by government-sponsored organizations such as the Federal National Mortgage Association (Fannie Mae) and the Federal Home Loan Banks.

Bankers' acceptance. Commercial notes guaranteed by a bank.

Certificates of deposit. Large-denomination, negotiable CDs sold by both U.S. and foreign commercial banks and by some S&Ls.

Commercial paper. IOUs sold by corporations for day-to-day operating funds.

Eurodollar CDs. Dollar-denominated certificates sold by foreign branches of U.S. banks or by foreign banks.

Treasury bills and notes. Sold on a periodic basis by the U.S. Treasury and backed by the "full faith and credit" of the government.

Repurchase agreements. "Repros," buy-sell deals in which the fund buys securities with an agreement that the seller will actually repurchase them within a short time—generally seven days or less —at a price that includes interest for that time. The fund holds the securities as collateral.

Yankee CDs. Certificates issued by U.S. branches of foreign banks.

FORMULA

This formula will determine if a tax-exempt money fund is worthwhile for you. Its value, of course, depends upon how much it will save you in taxes.

Divide the tax-exempt fund rate by that of a regular money fund, then subtract the result from the number 1. The final figure represents the minimum tax bracket for which investing in the tax-exempt fund provides an equal return.

For example, if the tax-exempt fund is paying 7 percent and the taxable fund 12 percent, then:

$$7 \text{ divided by } 12 = 0.58$$

$$1 \text{ minus } 0.58 = 0.42.$$

You would have to be in at least the 42 percent tax bracket for the tax-exempt fund to yield as much as the taxable fund.

---

10 Certificates of Deposit

Certificates of deposit, called **CDs**, are time certificates sold by banks. They are issued for a specified amount of money for a specified period. If you are looking for safety and high yields, this is the place for you. You agree to leave a certain amount of money with the bank, S&L, or credit union for a stated amount of time, ranging from a few months to several years.

Minimum deposits vary from several hundred dollars on up to several thousand dollars. Large CDs—those of $100,000 and up—are called **jumbo CDs**.

The Financial Services Revolution

CDs are part of the current "revolution in financial services," which can be said to have started in 1972 when the first money market mutual fund, The Reserve Fund, offered its shares to the public. Thus, the small investor got a taste of high interest rates for the first time. And for a minimum of only $1,000!

Until then, the only choices available to the investor with several hundred (or several thousand) dollars were a savings account and/or U.S. Savings Bonds—both paying measly returns.

For years, government rules made it virtually impossible for small savers to do much: Savings accounts had interest ceilings on them, and the higher-yielding commercial banks' CDs could be issued only in denominations of $100,000 or higher. Government restrictions prevented small depositors from pulling their money out of passbook savings accounts and putting it in CDs, because the feeling was that the banks might have trouble paying their many customers high CD market rates, since most of their assets at that time were in low-yielding mortgages. In the process of protecting the banks, the government was harshly penalizing the small saver.

As the money market funds began to make significant inroads, however, taking small savers away from the banks, these venerable institutions demanded that the government lift their interest rate ceilings, all of which led to today's far more competitive, and deregulated, banking environment.

Differences Among Bank CDs

Because all banks are now free to bid for your money, it is crucial that you investigate as many as possible when looking for a CD. Don't assume they all have more or less the same rates, because it's just not true. Minimums vary. Rates vary. Compounding interest varies. Maturities vary.

In general, you will find that:

- Interest rates on similar CDs offered by different banks in the same city can vary by as much as one full percentage point.

- You will earn more on your CD if the interest is compounded daily.

- Some banks "tier" their interest rates, which means they pay higher interest on larger deposits.

- Banks can set any maturities they wish.

- Many banks will let you set your own maturity for what they call a "designer CD." If you have to prepare for college tuition, for instance, you can buy a CD that comes due when your child goes off to school in September.

When shopping for a CD, ask your banker about his institution's policy regarding penalties for cashing in a certificate before it matures. The new rules stipulate that on deposits of one year or less, the penalty is thirty-one days' interest. On deposits of one year or more, it is ninety days' interest. Not all banks have dropped their penalties to the new minimums.

If you have an older CD, purchased before October 1983, the old regulations still apply. However, on the new insured CDs of thirty-two days or more, there is no legally imposed ceiling on the interest rate the bank can pay, and there is no legally imposed minimum.

Depending upon where you live, and the number of area banks competing for your money, you will find that CD minimums range from about $500 to $1,000. For those that will mature in less than a year, $1,000 to $2,500 is standard. CDs that remain on deposit for over a year are often available for only $500.

Again, we suggest you look for teddy bears and toasters. When banks need money, they are more apt to offer bonuses. For example, New York's Dollar Dry Dock Savings Bank permits savers to convert from a fixed- to a variable-rate CD after one or two years.* Manufacturers National Bank of Detroit will waive the annual credit card fee on Visa and MasterCharge for CDs of $5,000 or more. Watch for periodic local interest-rate wars and take advantage of temporarily higher rates.

CDS VERSUS OTHER CASH ALTERNATIVES

Vs. Money markets:
Although CDs of one year or less tend to pay slightly higher rates than bank money market accounts, you give up immediate access to your money.

Vs. Treasury notes:
Before you buy a longer-term CD, compare the rate to a Treasury note (see page 74). An advantage over T-notes is that their interest is free from state and local taxes.

Buying a CD from Your Broker

As part of the trend toward one-stop financial shopping, you can now buy a CD through a stockbroker. With a broker, you will get high yields as well as FDIC insurance, and you escape those hefty early-withdrawal penalties the banks impose.

When you buy a bank CD you agree to leave your money on deposit for a stated period—a few months to several years. If you want to get your money out, you have to pay a penalty.

If you are attracted by high interest and low minimum investment and yet want to avoid the early-withdrawal penalties, a brokered CD is probably the right move.

Here's how it works. *First,* you tell your broker what CD maturity you want. He will quote a rate. Since the bank pays the broker to sell the CD, you will not be stuck paying your broker a commission. Then you proceed to buy the CD.

Second, if you want to redeem it before maturity, you can sell it back to the broker without a penalty—he can readily sell it to

---

*A fixed-rate CD has an interest rate that remains the same until the CD matures. A variable-rate CD adjusts its interest periodically.

someone else in the "secondary market." However, the price of the CD will fluctuate depending upon what it's worth on the open market.

In general, your CD will go up in price if money market interest rates go down. It will decrease in value if money market interest rates rise. That means it is sometimes possible to make a profit by actually cashing in a CD early.

CHECKLIST

- Call two or three banks as well as your broker to see who has the highest rate.

- Ask how the interest is calculated. Daily, remember, is better than weekly.

- You may get a slightly higher rate at your broker's office because he buys huge certificates of $100,000 or more and then sells you a $1,000 chunk. These jumbo certificates pay higher interest rates than the smaller bank CDs.

- Make certain that the brokerage house will keep track of your CDs and mail you the interest if you like, or reinvest it if that is your wish.

Choosing a CD Interest Rate

Advertising by financial institutions may herald high rates in order to entice you and your money. But before you buy a certificate of deposit from a bank, read the fine print and figure out the interest rate.

- *Compounding.* Note whether the ad says interest is compounded or simple. Compounded is better because it means your interest earns interest. If compounded, is it done annually, semiannually, monthly, daily? It makes a difference. On a one-year certificate of deposit that pays 12 percent simple, interest is just that—12 percent. But when compounded daily, that 12 percent yields the equivalent of 12.94 percent over the course of a year.

- *Floating Rates.* Some accounts and CDs have floating rates in which interest is tied to an index, such as rates on U.S. Treasury securities. Banks should explain the initial rate, and most do, but they cannot tell you what the long-term rate will be, since it fluctuates.

- *Teaser Rates.* Some institutions offer a high introductory rate, which then drops. The high rate is apt to appear in the ads, the low rate in the fine print.

- *Annual Yields.* Often the yield given in an ad is for one year or less, and it assumes upon maturity* that you will reinvest all the money in another CD paying the same rate. In other words, if you don't roll over your CD, or if you roll it over into an account paying a lower rate, you won't get the advertised yield.

- *To Protect Yourself.* Ask your banker:
  1. What the interest rate will be during the entire life of a fixed rate
  2. What the effective annual yield is
  3. What the penalities are for early withdrawal

All interest rates are quoted on an annual basis.

PART FOUR

The
First $1,000

---

11 Investing for Income:Bonds

To safeguard your principal and at the same time guarantee long-term income, you can't beat bonds as a sure $1,000 investment.

Bond Basics

Simply stated, a bond (unlike a stock) is an IOU. When you purchase a bond you are, in effect, lending your money to the issuing company or government agency.* Bonds come in three types:

1. those issued by the U.S. Government and its agencies

2. those issued by corporations

3. those issued by states and municipalities, known as tax-exempt or "muni's."

---

*We will cover U.S. Government or Treasury bonds and notes in the next chapter.

The issuers of the bond are obligated to pay back the full purchase price at a particular time, and not before. This is called the **maturity date**. The reason people buy bonds is to receive a high secure rate of return (called interest) on their investment.

In general, bonds fall into two time-related categories: **intermediate notes** which mature in two to ten years; and **long-term bonds**, which mature or come due in ten years or longer.

Until your bond matures, you will be receiving a fixed rate of interest on your money. This is called the **coupon rate** and is usually paid out twice a year. For example, on a $1,000 bond that pays 10 percent (fixed rate), you will receive a $50 check every six months until maturity.

You may be interested to know that the term **coupon** dates from the time when all bonds actually came with a page of attached coupons. On each specified date, the owner of the bond clipped off the coupon, took it to the bank, and exchanged it for cash. This procedure still holds for Treasury bonds.

The **face value** or denomination of a bond is also known as **par value** and is usually $1,000. That means bonds are sold at $1,000 when they are first issued. After that their price may vary, moving up and down just as stocks do. Depending upon the prevailing market conditions, bonds are sold or traded either *above par* (that is, above $1,000), which is also called **at premium**; or **below par**, which is less than $1,000 and also called **at a discount.**.

And, just to make it a bit more confusing, although bonds are issued and sold in $1,000 units, their prices in the newspaper and elsewhere are quoted on the basis of $100, not $1,000. So you must always add a zero to the price. For example, a bond quoted at $105 is really selling for $1,050. (See section entitled Price and Yield which follows.)

Buying New or Old Bonds

When buying bonds you can either buy a **new issue**, in which case the issuing company pays the broker's fee; or, you can buy an **older bond** on the open market, in which case *you* pay a commission. New bonds are those issued for the first time to the public. Old bonds are those that someone purchased, held, and then decided to sell before maturity.

After bonds have been issued, *they do not stay at the same price*. They rise and fall in price depending upon supply and demand and upon availability of new bonds that give buyers a higher interest rate or a lower interest rate. If new bonds pay more interest, then older bonds drop in price. If new bonds pay less interest, then older bonds rise in price because they are more desirable.

It is possible to sell your bond before maturity, although the issuer is not obliged to redeem it ahead of time. Investors can almost always sell a bond in the open market through a stockbroker—but it is possible you will not receive what you paid for it, the price being more or less dependent upon the market.

The minimum bond investment is usually $5,000 to $10,000 through brokers. But it is indeed possible to enter the bond market by buying a single $1,000 bond through a stockbroker. You can buy a bond mutual fund or a unit investment trust for $1,000. These vehicles are explained on pages 66–70.

Price and Yield

Just like stock prices, bond prices fluctuate. Their market value changes every day (or several times a day) in reaction to the availability of our number-one commodity: money. As interest rates go up or down, bond prices change. This is due to the fact that the bond coupon or interest rate is set; so the only way the bond market can accommodate to changes in interest rates is by changing the bond's current market price.

It works like this:

- When interest rates go down, bond prices go up.

- When interest rates go up, bond prices fall.

The rule of thumb to keep in mind is: *Bond prices move in exactly the opposite direction from interest rates.*

Let's say you buy a $1,000 bond at 10 percent, which means $100 annually in interest payments. If interest rates move up and the same corporation issues new bonds, it might do so at 10½ percent, or $105 per year. The impact then on the corporation's older bond (the one you own) would be as follows:

- Although its relative value will fall somewhat, the interest, or coupon, rate will remain the same. But the bond's selling price could drop to around $960, where the yield would then approximate 10½ percent.*

---

*Yield is the equivalent of 10½ percent on a $1,000 bond, because of the $40 you save by buying the bond for $960.

Now let's look at the same situation when interest rates fall to 9½ percent. Then the corporation issues new bonds at the lower coupon rate. In this case the older bond (the one you purchased) will rise in value. Thus a 10 percent bond could sell at $105, that is 10 divided by $105 = 9.5 percent.

If you need to raise money and sell your $1,000 bond at $960 and take a $40 loss, someone else may buy it and hold it until maturity, when it will be worth $1,000, making a $40 profit. The total return to that person, including both the interest and the gain in price, is called the **yield to maturity**.

Bonds and the Risk Element

In order to determine a bond's safety, you can consult one of the professional rating services—either Standard & Poor's or Moody's. Their rating books are on the shelves of most public libraries or at your broker's office. The highest rating is triple A. Medium-grade bonds fall into the triple B category, while those that are C or lower are speculative. In general, inexperienced investors should stick with bonds rated A or better.

Moody's		S&P
Aaa	Top quality	AAA
Aa	Excellent	AA
A	Very high	A
Baa	Medium	BBB
Ba	Speculative	BB
B	Lower speculative	B
Caa	Poor & risky	CCC
Ca	Near default	CC
C	In default	C

The two key risk factors are:

- If you must sell before maturity, interest rates may have climbed, making your bond worth less. This has been historically true during the inflationary period of the last decade.

- Your bonds may be "called in." Most bonds have **call features**, which give the issuer the right to redeem the bond before maturity. The conditions for calling in a bond are given in the statement filed with the SEC when the bonds are first issued to the public.

The call feature is usually not exercised if the current interest rate is the same or higher than the bond coupon rate. But, if interest rates fall below the bond coupon rate, it is sometimes likely that the bond will be called because now the issuer can borrow money somewhere else at a lower rate. (Remember, a bond is just a loan you make to the issuer, who would naturally prefer to pay the lowest interest rate possible.)

Call Protection

If a bond is called in, you then, of course, lose that steady stream of income you thought you had locked in for a given number of years. But there is a way to protect yourself from calls, and it is especially essential when investing long term. You can buy a bond with "call protection," which guarantees that it will not be called for a specific number of years. Corporate bonds are likely to offer ten-year call protection. Most government bonds are not callable at all.

Who Issues Bonds?

We will cover U.S. Government, or Treasury, bonds and notes (see Chapter 12), and municipal bonds (see pages 63–66). Let's look at corporate bonds now.

Corporate Bonds

Thousands of large U.S. corporations raise money by selling bonds to the public. Some of these companies are small and obscure; others are well known. In general, it is best to stick to the bonds of leading companies, because if you need to sell your bonds to raise cash, you can do so more easily. Look for bonds traded on the New York Stock Exchange. Bond prices and yields are listed in a special section of the newspaper. **Corporate bonds** can be purchased from a stockbroker in $1,000 face value denominations.

Prices for bonds are quoted in the newspaper with fractions

listed in eighths. For example, a bond listed at $98¼ is really selling for $982.50. Here's what a typical listing looks like:

Bond	Current Yield	Sales in $1,000	High	Low	Last	Net Change
duPont 14s91	13	249	105	103⅞	104½	+ ½

The first column indicates that this E.I. duPont Corporation bond has a coupon rate of 14 percent and a maturity date of 1991. In other words, it pays $140 per year for every $1,000 bond. If you divide the coupon rate (14 percent) by the current market price (which is listed under "Last" and is $104½), you will get the current yield (which is 13 percent). The volume of bonds traded was 249 bonds. The high was $1,050 and the low $1,038.75. The closing price was $1,045, up $5 per bond.

You may wonder why the yield for this bond fell from 14 percent to 13 percent. The answer is that the price of the bond has gone up from $1,000, which it was on the first day it was issued, to $1,050.

Are Corporate Bonds for You?

Yes, if you stick with those with top ratings. These could include such well-known corporations as General Motors, Exxon, Xerox, IBM, General Electric, and duPont. But remember, unlike government bonds (see Chapter 12), corporate bonds are not guaranteed. Your protection is the financial strength of the corporation. And, *the greater the financial strength of the issuer, the lower the coupon or interest rate, because safety is traded off for lower yields.*

CORPORATE BONDS

For Whom

- Anyone seeking high fixed income who also accepts the risk of a changing interest-rate market

Safety Factor

- Can be determined by bond ratings, with AAA and AA being the highest ratings

- Does vary depending upon the corporation
- Are not insured or guaranteed

Minimum Investment

- $1,000

Advantages

- Corporate bonds almost always pay higher interest rates than government bonds or those issued by municipalities.
- You can select bonds to come due when you need your principal repaid.
- Corporate bonds are a good way of investing for income.

Disadvantages

- Many bonds have call provisions.
- There is a lack of liquidity.
- Interest income is subject to federal, state, and local taxes.
- There is generally no appreciation of principal as there is with stocks.

Special Hint: Unless you are experienced, you are better off playing with corporate bonds through a corporate bond mutual fund or unit trust because the bonds are professionally selected and managed (see page 66–70).

Municipal Bonds

Municipal bonds are desirable for those investors seeking interest income that is exempt from income tax because of the tax bracket they are in—30 percent or higher. (See chart on page 65 to determine if you would benefit from municipals.)

By far the largest number of bonds offered are tax-exempt or municipal bonds. These are issued by cities, counties, states, and by special agencies to finance various projects. Their biggest plus: Interest paid is exempt from federal income tax and state and local taxes in the area where issued. (If, however, you buy municipals of another state, they will be subject to taxes in your state.) Because of the tax advantage, municipal bonds pay lower interest rates than comparable corporate bonds or government securities. Your interest and principal are re-paid to you by taxes and revenues collected by the municipalities.

Municipal bond dealers and the major retail brokers such as Merrill Lynch, E.F. Hutton, or Prudential Bache are interested in working only with customers who have a minimum of $25,000 to invest in these bonds. Smaller investors, however, can participate through purchasing unit investment trusts or municipal bond funds, which are explained on pages 67–68.

How to Select Tax-Exempts

There are three factors to check when considering tax-exempt bonds: *safety*, *yield*, and *liquidity*. You can check the safety of any bond, tax-exempt or not, through Moody's or Standard & Poor's rating services. In addition to sticking to A-rated bonds, you can increase your safety factor by:

- Buying bonds that come with a federal government guarantee

- Buying bonds that are insured

There are several private concerns that insure bonds, among them American Municipal Bond Assurance Corporation and Municipal Bond Insurance Association. Because there have been a few cases of municipal bonds that have defaulted (the best-known example recently being the Washington Public Power System), insured bonds are a sound idea.

In order to insure a bond, the issuer pays an insurance premium that ranges from 0.1 percent to 2 percent of total principal and interest. The insurance company then agrees to pay both the principal and the interest to bondholders if the issuer defaults. Policies generally last the life of the bond. You will find that insured bonds have slightly lower yields, for obvious reasons.

The second factor in municipal bond selection is *yield*. Tax-exempts, as we mentioned before, pay lower interest rates than most taxable bonds and therefore are not appropriate for people in low tax brackets or for placement in already tax-deferred retirement accounts.

In order to determine whether or not you would benefit from owning municipals, find your spot on the Tax Exempt/Taxable

Yield Equivalents chart. It illustrates the fact that tax-exempt securities can increase the *after-tax income* of an investor who is in the 30 percent tax bracket or above. You can see, for example, that a single person with a taxable income of $30,000 would need to earn more than 15 percent on a taxable security in order to match a 10 percent yield on a tax-exempt security.

TAX EXEMPT/TAXABLE YIELD EQUIVALENTS

(Individual income brackets—thousands of dollars)

Single Return ($000)	$23.5 to $28.8		$28.8 to $34.1	$34.1 to $41.5	$41.5 to $55.3		$58.3 to $81.8		over $81.8
Joint Return ($000)	$29.9 to $35.2		$35.2 to $45.8		$45.8 to $60.0	$60.0 to $85.6	$85.6 to $109.4		$109.4 to $162.4	to $162.4
Tax Bracket	28%	30%	33%	34%	38%	42%	45%	48%	49%	50%
Tax Exempt Yields (%) 6.0	8.3	8.5	8.9	9.0	9.6	10.3	10.9	11.5	11.7	12.0
7.0	9.7	10.0	10.4	10.6	11.2	12.0	12.7	13.4	13.7	14.0
7.5	10.4	10.7	11.1	11.3	12.0	12.9	13.6	14.4	14.7	15.0
8.0	11.1	11.4	11.9	12.1	12.9	13.8	14.5	15.4	15.7	16.0
8.5	11.8	12.1	12.6	12.8	13.7	14.6	15.4	16.3	16.6	17.0
9.0	12.5	12.9	13.4	13.6	14.5	15.5	16.4	17.3	17.6	18.0
9.5	13.2	13.6	14.2	14.4	15.3	16.4	17.3	18.3	18.6	19.0
10.0	13.9	14.3	14.9	15.2	16.1	17.2	18.2	19.2	19.6	20.0
10.5	14.6	15.0	15.7	15.9	16.9	18.1	19.1	20.2	20.6	21.0
11.0	15.3	15.7	16.4	16.7	17.7	19.0	20.0	21.2	21.6	22.0
11.5	16.0	16.4	17.2	17.4	18.5	19.8	20.9	22.1	22.5	23.0
12.0	16.7	17.1	17.9	18.2	19.4	20.7	21.8	23.1	23.5	24.0
12.5	17.4	17.9	18.7	18.9	20.2	21.6	22.7	24.0	24.5	25.0
13.0	18.1	18.6	19.4	19.7	21.0	22.4	23.6	25.0	25.5	26.0
13.5	18.8	19.3	20.1	20.5	21.8	23.3	24.5	26.0	26.5	27.0
14.0	19.4	20.0	20.9	21.2	22.6	24.1	25.5	26.9	27.5	28.0
14.5	20.1	20.7	21.6	22.0	23.4	25.0	26.4	27.9	28.4	29.0
15.0	20.8	21.4	22.4	22.7	24.2	25.9	27.3	28.8	29.4	30.0

1984 Tax Year

The third factor involved in municipal bond selection is liquidity; that is, the ability to find someone who wants to buy your bond. It is best to stick with bonds of large, well-known municipalities or state governments. If you want to sell an obligation of the Moorland, Iowa, School District, it may be weeks before you find a dealer willing to buy these obscure bonds.

You can also avoid the liquidity problem by buying a tax-exempt unit trust or a bond mutual fund. We will explain these two investment packages next.

Special Hint: To avoid paying state taxes on a municipal bond, buy only those bonds that are issued in your own state and/or those issued in Puerto Rico. State governments regard Puerto Rico as if it were a part of the federal government and therefore free of state taxes.

For additional information on insured municipal bonds, write to:
Municipal Bond Assurance Corporation
1 State Street Plaza
New York, NY 10004

Bond Mutual Funds

The small-bond investor can buy into a bond fund or unit investment trust, in which you spread out your risk through participation in large, diversified portfolios of bonds that are professionally selected. There are two types of bond funds: **managed bond mutual funds** and **closed-end unit investment trusts**. You need to know about both.

The Managed Bond Mutual Fund

If you have $1,000 to $5,000 and want the advantages of diversification and professional management, you should consider this type of fund. As is the case with any other mutual fund (see page 9 and Chapter 9), in a bond fund you purchase shares of a professionally managed portfolio. The manager periodically reviews the contents of the fund's portfolio and makes buy-and-sell decisions based on performance and market conditions. Most funds have a minimum investment requirement of $1,000 and offer both convenience and diversification. Interest is automatically reinvested unless you give directions to the contrary; and an increasing number of bond funds allow you to write checks, usually a minimum of $500, against the value of your shares.

Bond funds come in two varieties: **load funds** and **no-load funds**. Those with a load are sold through stockbrokers and have a sales charge of as much as 8 percent of your initial investment. No-load funds are bought directly from management and are free of a sales charge. Since there is no proven difference in performance between a load and no-load fund, you might as well buy shares in a no-load fund.

If you ever wish to sell, the fund will buy back your shares at the current market price, which could be more or less than what you originally paid.

Tax-Exempt Unit Trusts

For those who wish to lock in a fixed tax-exempt yield, a **unit trust** is ideal. This also requires a minimum investment of $1,000 per unit. These are set up by big brokerage houses and bond dealers who buy several million dollars' worth of bonds and then sell them to individual investors in $1,000 pieces. You pay the broker a one-time fixed fee, about 7 percent to 8 percent of the value of the units.

Unit trusts are prepackaged, diversified portfolios of tax-exempt bonds that lock in a specific, unchanging yield. Unlike bond mutual funds, they are "unmanaged:" they are "closed-end" trusts —in other words, once the bonds for the trust have been selected, no new issues are added—ever. (Issues that turn out to be a problem, however, can be sold in order to minimize losses.) The trust gradually liquidates itself as the bonds mature; until then, the unit price fluctuates with prevailing interest rates.

When you buy a unit trust, you are buying a share of a larger portfolio. This has the advantage of reducing your risk through diversification—by spreading out your investment dollars over twenty or thirty bonds. A trust has the added plus of professional selection. The average investor does not have time to sort through hundreds of bond prospectuses and then check each one's credit rating. The bond trust does this for you (so does the bond mutual fund).

Nevertheless, neither diversification nor professional management completely erases the risk factor. Bond prices fall when interest rates rise and rise when interest rates fall; so will unit trust prices rise and fall with changes in interest rates.

The concept behind the unit investment trust is that if you hold on to it until maturity, you will then get back your initial investment. Maturity can be ten, twenty, or even thirty-plus years, depending upon the trust. In the interim, you will receive a fixed amount of tax-free income, usually on a monthly basis.

If you do not wish to hold the trust until maturity, you can sell it at any time in a "secondary market" either to the sponsor or to another broker. What you get back will depend upon the market. If interest rates have fallen, you will get more; but if they've gone up, it's possible that you may not even get back your original price.

Generous tax-exempt yields make unit trusts attractive. A couple earning $35,200 to $45,800—the 33 percent tax bracket—would have to earn 15.67 percent from a taxable investment to equal a 10.5 percent return from a municipal tax-free unit trust investment.

Trusts are ideal for those investors who wish to spend less than $25,000. They offer the investor with a limited amount of money a way to get into the action at an affordable price and hold a diversified portfolio.

Tax-Exempt Bond Mutual Funds

The investor seeking tax-exempt income has this alternative to the closed-end exempt unit trust. These are **managed mutual funds** in which the entire portfolio is made up of tax-exempt municipal bonds. They are available for a minimum investment of $1,000 and operate like any other managed mutual fund—that is, the management buys and sells securities in order to maximize the fund's yield.

Here's how to determine which one is for you:

- In a unit trust (tax exempt) the basic investment is fixed; no trading activity is conducted after initial bond purchases are made by the trust.

- In a tax-exempt bond fund, investments are bought and sold in order to maximize a high tax-exempt income.

- Sometimes bond funds perform better than fixed trusts, and vice versa. The key difference is not so much performance as the expenses involved.

- Unit trust sponsors take most of their fee up front when you buy. It ranges up to 8 percent of your purchase.

- Most, but not all, bond funds do not charge the investor a fee for buying or selling shares. They take about ½ percent to 1 percent of the annual income of the fund for expenses.

Single State Trusts

The best unit trust is often a **single state trust**. It contains bonds that have a triple tax exemption—that is, they are free from federal, state, and local taxes. You can buy them from regional brokers, large brokerage firms, and bond specialists. They contain portfolios of good-quality tax-free bonds issued for a variety of public purposes within a single state.

In addition to the large brokerage houses, there are several companies that sponsor single state trusts. You can contact them for further information. These include:

- John Nuveen & Company, which regularly issues new single state trusts. Its Multi-State Trust Series is available in Arizona, California, Colorado, Connecticut, Florida, Georgia, Maryland, Massachusetts, Michigan, Minnesota, New Jersey, New

York, North Carolina, Ohio, Pennsylvania, Texas, and Virginia.* For additional data contact:

John Nuveen & Company
61 Broadway
New York, NY 10006
212-668-9500

or

209 South LaSalle Street
Chicago, IL 60604
312-621-3000

- Van Kampen Merritt offers a variety of triple-exempt trusts:
Van Kampen Merritt
2 Penn Plaza
Philadelphia, PA 19102

800-523-4556
215-972-0555

- L.F. Rothschild Unterberg Towbin cosponsors with Smith Barney Harris Upham single state trusts for residents of New York City and New York Sate. Contact:
L.F. Rothschild, Unterberg, Towbin
55 Water Street
New York, NY 10041

Before you buy any municipal bond mutual fund or unit trust, take time to read the prospectus. Know what securities it contains, what their ratings are, and when you will receive your interest or dividend payments. Check out the various fees and charges, too. Don't leave yourself open for any hidden surprises.

Zero Coupon Bonds

If you will need money for college tuition, retirement, or to meet some other long-term financial goal, **zero coupon bonds** offer a

---

*The Municipal Investment Trust Funds, which have triple-exempt unit trusts for residents of New York, California, Pennsylvania, Maryland, Minnesota, and Michigan, are cosponsored by Merrill Lynch, Dean Witter, Shearson/American Express, and Prudential Bache. Contact the local office of any one of these brokers.

viable solution, because you make a small investment today and get a large balloon payment in the future.

A "zero," unlike regular bonds, pays zero interest until maturity. To compensate for this fact, it is sold at a deep discount, well below the $1,000 standard bond price, and it increases in value at a compound rate so that by maturity it is worth much more than when you bought it. Although this type of bond does not pay interest along the way, you will be taxed annually by the IRS as though it did, because the government wants to collect the tax due along the way.

Here's an example of a recent zero: A $1,000 zero that yields 11.9 percent and matures in twenty years will sell for only $85.40. In other words, you invest $85.40 at 11.9 percent today. 11.9 percent interest is paid on your investment and the reinvested interest, and after twenty years your $85.40 will equal $1,000. Interest "turns into" principal, and is paid to you in a lump sum upon maturity.

As you can see, with a zero coupon bond you know ahead of time exactly how much money you will have when the bond comes due. Yet because zeros, unlike regular bonds, lock in interest, you get a slightly lower yield, about ½ to 1 percentage point below bonds that have a regular coupon. (See page 58 for an explanation of coupons.)

There are four types of zeros.

1. *Corporate Zeros* are issued by large corporations. The very first zero, in fact, was issued by J.C. Penney in 1981. Offered at $250 each, they mature in 1992, when they will be worth $1,000. That works out to a 13.5 percent yield. Because they are a long-term investment, you need to have faith in the corporation and its credit worthiness.

2. *Treasury Zeros* are packaged and sold by large brokerage and investment houses. These institutions buy huge lots of long-term U.S. Treasury bonds, clip off (or "strip off") the semiannual interest coupons, then sell these coupons, which come due twice a year during the life of the bond. Each package guarantees that the buyer of these coupons will get $1,000 upon maturity. Principal and interest are guaranteed by the U.S. Government. These "strip bonds," as they are called, are also known by various names: Merrill Lynch sells TIGERs which stands for Treasury Investment Growth Re-

ceipt; Salomon Brothers' CATS are Certificates of Accrual on Treasury Securities and are available through Prudential-Bache; and LIONs, Lehman Investment Opportunity Notes, are sold through Lehman Brothers Kuhn Loeb.

Recent examples:
1. A six-year Treasury zero yielding 11.38 percent sold for $474.
2. A twelve-year zero yielding 11.42 percent sold for $342.
3. An eighteen-year zero yielding 11.07 percent sold for $132.

3. *Tax-Exempt Zeros* are issued by municipalities, states, and other agencies. Just as with other municipal bonds, their interest is exempt from federal income tax and from state and local tax in the issuing community. Like other tax-exempt bonds, they pay a lower rate.

4. *Zero Coupon CDs* are similar to zero coupon bonds. They are obligations of large banks and, like bank deposits, are insured up to $100,000 by the FDIC.

ZERO COUPON BONDS

For Whom

- Those who know they will need a certain amount of money at a certain time in the future

Minimum

- Varies; never less than $100

Safety Factor

- Minimal risk

Advantages

- You know precisely how much you must invest now to get a certain amount of money on a certain date in the future.

- You do not have to be concerned with the reinvestment of interest payments as is the case with regular bonds.

Disadvantages

- When interest rates rise, the value of the zeros you hold falls even more than the value of regular bonds, because, since you have no cash in hand from interest payments, you cannot take a zero's interest and reinvest it at a higher rate elsewhere.

- Yields are ½ to 1 percentage point below ordinary bonds.

- The IRS insists that taxes be paid annually on zero coupon bonds just as if you actually received the interest.

- You are paying taxes on theoretical interest even though no cash is received until the date of maturity. The buyer of a regular bond pays taxes, too, but he also receives interest payments in the form of cash twice a year.

Special Hint: If you do not want to get locked into the lower yield of a longer-term zero coupon bond because you fear inflation and the higher interest rates it brings, buy zeros with shorter maturities.

HOW TO BUILD A COLLEGE FUND WITH ZEROS

Recently a grandmother attending the first birthday celebration of her granddaughter announced a gift of $10,000 toward the little girl's college education, which would start in 2003. Her cost for this $10,000 was only $1,060, because she had purchased zero coupon bonds from her broker that were due to mature then.

You, too, can use zero coupon bonds to prepare for the day when your child or grandchild goes to college.

- Select zeros scheduled to come due at the right time.

- Then, to reduce taxes, set up a custodial account through your broker or banker. This type of account holds money, stocks, or bonds in a parent's name for the child until he or she is of age. Interest will be taxed at the child's lower tax bracket level. On interest up to $1,000 a year there is no tax and between $1,000 and $6,000 a year the tax rate varies from 12 percent to 16 percent.

- See your broker or banker for the proper forms to fill out.

12 U.S. Treasury Notes & Bonds

When you have accumulated an extra $1,000 or more, it's time to consider one of the safest of all investment vehicles— **Treasuries**, which is Wall Street-eze for securities issued by the U.S. Government. Long regarded as an ideal place for a portion of anyone's savings, these investments have three things in their favor:

- They are the safest form of investment because the U.S. Government guarantees to pay you back.

- They are extremely liquid and can be sold at any time.

- Interest earned is exempt from state and local taxes.

Where do Treasuries come from? Uncle Sam constantly borrows money, not only to finance building battleships but also to cover the high federal deficit, by issuing short-term Treasury bills and longer-term notes and bonds. (The difference among all three —bills, notes, and bonds—is the time limit or maturity. They run from a minimum of thirteen weeks to a maximum of thirty years.)

- **Treasury bills** mature in a year or less. They come in 13-, 26-, and 52-week maturities and require a minimum investment of $10,000. Instead of paying interest, they are sold below face value—that is, at a discount.

- **Treasury notes** mature in two to ten years and require a minimum investment of $5,000 for those maturing in less than four years, and $1,000 for those maturing in more than four years.

- **Treasury bonds** mature in ten years or more; the minimum investment is $1,000.

So, for the highest safety rating you generally must accept a comparatively low interest rate; however, since the government has to finance a 1984 deficit of $183 billion, a number of new issues have recently flooded the market and yields are now high.

Most corporate and municipal bonds have a call feature (see Chapter 11). This means that the issuer has the privilege of redeeming the bonds prior to maturity. In other words, issuers of bonds have a right to "call" in or redeem a bond at a specific date for cash. Redemption prices are determined and the call year stated when the bond is initially offered to the public. All Treasury notes and most Treasury bonds are not callable. This is an advantage of Treasuries in addition to their safety and exemption from state and local taxes.

What About Yields?

Yields on Treasuries vary, depending upon the supply and demand of money. This means that when money is tight the yield will tend to be higher than when it's more readily available. When you invest in a Treasury you must realize that you won't know the precise yield until it is set at auction. Yields are decided by an auction. Public auctions are held periodically by the U.S. Treasury for major banks and government bond dealers. The public may also participate (we will tell you how in a bit).

Both notes and bonds have a "par" value of 100, which means 100 percent of the face amount—$1,000. Although the interest rate is fixed and set by the Treasury auction, notes and bonds can sell above par or below par, that is, above $1,000 or below $1,000.

If they sell above par, you will pay a premium, and the effective yield will be less than the interest rate printed on the bond. For example, if you buy a 10 percent bond and you pay $1,030 you are paying above par, or at a premium.

$$\frac{\text{10 percent (the interest rate printed on the bond)}}{\text{\$1,030 (the price you paid for a \$1,000 bond)}} = \text{9.7 percent (the effective yield)}$$

which is lower than 10 percent. Treasuries also have a coupon rate, a term left over from the days when bonds had an attached page of coupons; on the set date the owner of the bond clipped the coupon and took it to his bank to exchange for the interest earned in cash (see Chapter 11).

If the bond sells below par, it is selling at a discount, and the effective yield will be higher than the coupon rate. For example, if you buy a 10 percent bond and you pay $970, then you're buying it at a discount or below par.

$$\frac{10 \text{ percent}}{\$970} = \text{an effective yield of 10.3 percent}$$

How to Become Part of the Auction

You can buy Treasuries at the auction through a broker or your bank, for around $25 per order. But there's no need to do so, because you can also buy them through the mail or from the Federal Reserve Bank or the Bureau of Public Debt in your area. (There are twelve Federal Reserve districts, each with a main bank and thirty-seven additional branches.) When the U.S. Treasury holds an auction in which large banks and government bond dealers bid for notes, bills, and bonds, their bids are actually placed through the Federal Reserve Banking system (see list on page 79–80).

Auctions for Treasuries are announced. *The Wall Street Journal* and other newspapers provide this material, or you can call your district Federal Reserve office and get a copy of their newsletter, *Highlights of Treasury Offerings*, which contains a list of auction dates.

The auctions have a regular schedule for the most part. In general:

- Thirteen- and twenty-six-week bills are auctioned every Monday.

- 52-week bills are auctioned once a month.

- 2-year notes are auctioned once a month.

- 3-year and longer notes are auctioned every three months.

- Bonds are auctioned every three months.

Bidding

In order to get into the auction you will need to enter a bid, which is also called submitting a tender. The Treasury provides a specific form, but if you don't have one you can also write a letter with your bid. (For a copy of the Treasury form, contact your nearest Federal Reserve Bank; the address is available from your own local bank.) This is how it works: The Treasury announces the maturity date a week before the auction. The auction is then held to determine the interest rate or yield the bidders will accept for that specific maturity. In other words, bids are in yields, not prices.

If you decide to purchase a bill, bond, or note by mail, you must provide payment for the full face value of the bill, note, or bond and include the following facts in your letter:

- Your name, address and telephone number

- Your Social Security number or taxpayer ID

- The amount, type, and maturity of the security you want to purchase

- In whose name you want the security registered

- Their names and Social Security numbers if it's a trust for a minor or to be held in joint names

- For bills, state if you want the funds reinvested in new bills upon maturity

- Your signature

- Your payment

- If the bid is competitive or not (if you will accept the average auction price or will limit your bid to a certain interest rate)

- A completed IRS W-9 form

On the outside of the envelope, which is addressed to your nearest Federal Reserve Bank, type or write: "Tender for Treasury Notes (or Bonds)."

Your tender to buy must be entered by the deadline, which is 1:00 P.M. Eastern time on the day of the auction. Or, you can even go in person to the Federal Reserve Bank and fill out a form there, presenting your payment to the cashier. Government regulations insist that payment be *in cash*:

Mail to: Bureau of Public Debt or to: The Federal Reserve Bank
              Securities Transaction   in your area
              Branch
              Room 2134, Main Treasury
              Washington, DC 20226

Payment may be in the form of a certified personal check made out to the Federal Reserve Bank or the U.S. Treasury, or you may use already matured Treasury notes or bonds.

Bids can be competitive or noncompetitive. If your bid is competitive, then you must state in your letter the rate you will accept written out to two decimal points: for example, 10.75 percent. With a noncompetitive tender, you, the tender, agree to pay the average of the competitive bids accepted by the Treasury.

Competitive bids are usually entered only by the "big guns"— the institutional buyers such as banks, mutual funds, pension funds, insurance companies, and so forth. The average public investor generally puts in a noncompetitive bid in order to avoid being shut out by bidding too high or too low. (Keep in mind that bids are yields, not prices.)

Then, the average bid is generally announced that evening and appears in the next morning's newspaper. If there's any difference between your bid (if you put in a competitive bid) and the final yield, you will receive notice of the fact from the Treasury. They will either bill you or send you a check.

After the Auction

Using Your Broker

After the auction is over you can buy and sell Treasury notes, bonds, and bills through your broker.

If you have an account at a brokerage house, your broker will act as your purchasing agent. Regular commissions are charged on orders. The broker's fee will vary from firm to firm, ranging from $10 to $35 for orders of any size. Some brokers charge $2.50 or $3.00 per $1,000, with a minimum of $35 or $40. Others have a flat fee—maybe $50, $75, or $100, regardless of the size of the order.

Most brokers buy Treasuries primarily as a service to their clients, because they do not make much on the transaction.

A few discount brokers will also buy Treasuries. It is worth calling several in your area because the cost to you will be much lower than with a full-service broker.

Going Through a Bank

Banks that are a part of the Federal Reserve System will buy Treasuries, for a fee—or retail markup. Many banks will keep the security for you and mail you the interest. Monthly safekeeping fees run approximately $1 to $3.

Before having either your bank or your broker handle purchase of Treasuries, however, check out the fees, both the obvious ones and any that may be hidden. If you decide to hold the securities yourself, ask what the transfer fee is. Some institutions charge as much as $75 for each certificate delivered to you. Shop around.

THE TWELVE FEDERAL RESERVE BANKS

Boston
600 Atlantic Avenue
Boston, MA 02106
617-973-3800

New York
33 Liberty Street
Federal Reserve P.O. Station
New York, NY 10045
212-791-5823

Richmond
P.O. Box 27622
Richmond, VA 23261
804-643-1250

Philadelphia
100 North Sixth Street
P.O. Box 66
Philadelphia, PA 19105
215-574-6580

Cleveland
1455 East Sixth Street
P.O. Box 6387
Cleveland, OH 44101
216-579-2490

Atlanta
P.O. Box 1731
Atlanta, GA 30301
404-586-8657

Chicago
230 South La Salle Street
P.O. Box 834
Chicago, IL 60690
312-786-1110

Minneapolis
250 Marquette Avenue
Minneapolis, MN 55480
612-340-2051

Dallas
400 South Akard Street
Station K
Dallas, TX 75222
214-651-6177

St. Louis
411 Locust Street
P.O. Box 442
St. Louis, MO 63166
314-444-8444

Kansas City
925 Grand Avenue
Federal Reserve Station
Kansas City, MO 63166
816-881-2738

San Francisco
P.O. Box 7702
San Francisco, CA 94120
415-392-6639

U.S. TREASURIES

For Whom

- Investors seeking absolute safety
- Those with a minimum of $1,000
- Those who enjoy helping Uncle Sam

Fee

- There is no fee if ordered directly from the Federal Reserve.
- Banks and brokers charge various fees, ranging from a few dollars to as high as $50 or $75.

Safety Factor

- The highest possible
- Backed by the U.S. government

Advantages

- Principal and interest are guaranteed against default.

- You can sell Treasuries through a broker before maturity without loss because interest accrues daily until date of your sale.

- Maximum liquidity

- The state and local tax exemption makes Treasuries especially attractive for those who live in a state with high taxes.

Disadvantages

- Troublesome to purchase unless you pay the fee and use your bank or broker.

Hint: Buying a bank CD is easier and generally pays about the same interest or a little less.

TREASURY TELEPHONE HELP

Call: 202-287-4088   A continuous recorded message with information on Treasury Notes and Bonds

202-287-4100   A continuous recorded message with prices and yields of the most recently sold securities plus information on those being offered for sale by the Treasury

202-287-4113   A recorded message with general information on how to order Treasuries by mail and a listing of other important data and telephone numbers. At the end of the recorded announcement, an analyst will answer your specific questions.

202-287-4217   A recorded message on how to buy Treasuries in person in Washington, DC, or through the mail.

Most of the Federal Reserve Banks (listed on pages 79–80) have recorded announcements with similar details. Pamphlets and other material on Treasuries are available from: Bureau of Public Debt, Dept. F, Washington, DC 20239-0001.

You may also be interested in the following free publications:

Basic Information on Treasury Bills
Federal Reserve Bank of New York
Public Information Department
33 Liberty Street
New York, NY 10045

Buying Treasury Securities at Federal Reserve Banks
Federal Reserve Bank of Richmond
Bank & Public Relations Department
P.O. Box 2762
Richmond, VA 23262

U.S. Financial Data
(a weekly newsletter)
Federal Reserve Bank of St. Louis
P.O. Box 442
St. Louis, MO 63166

There are two newsletters available for purchase that cover Treasuries:

Grant's Interest Rate Observer
233 Broadway
Suite 1216
New York, NY 10279
Published twice a month: $200/year

The Treasury Securities Market Report
Howard M. Berlin, Ltd.
P.O. Box 9431
Wilmington, DE 19809
Published monthly: $125/year or $75/six months
Includes a free copy of *The Dow Jones-Irwin Guide to Buying and Selling Securities*

Special Hints:

- Competitive bidding on Treasuries is a skilled art and should not be attempted by the average investor.

- Since you have to pay the Treasury in advance of the auction, you will lose some interest if your money was in an interest-bearing account or a money market fund. The U.S. Treasury deposits checks very quickly—usually within twenty-four hours. If you can, buy Treasuries in person. In that way your money is out only one or two days.

- It is easier to sell your Treasuries if you buy through a broker or commercial bank. You merely phone in your sell order—but, you then must pay the commission.

- If you buy directly from the government, in order to sell you must go to a bank or broker. You cannot sell Treasuries back to the government. And you must also fill out form PD 4633, "Request for Transactions in Book-Entry Treasury Bills Maintained by the Bureau of Public Debt." This document allows you to transfer the Treasury to a bank or broker who will then sell it in the open market.

- When sold in the open market, Treasuries—just like stocks—can be sold for more or less than their original price, depending upon the market. If, however, you hold the Treasury until maturity, you will get back the full amount you invested.

13 Stock Mutual Funds

Buying shares in a mutual fund is often a good alternative to trying to pick from among the thousands of stocks available. For the small investor, the new investor, and the very busy investor, mutual funds offer diversity, professional management, liquidity, and relatively low cost. Compared with other similar investments, they also offer the possibility of price appreciation. Some funds have no minimum investment amount; for others it is as low as $100. You should have at least $1,000 before you participate in a fund for stocks, however, because in this type of investment there is a greater degree of risk than in money market mutual funds,

CDs, and other vehicles we have already described. After all, the stock market, and your fund, could go down, not up, in price. That is the risk you take when purchasing a stock fund.

When you buy into a mutual fund you are actually purchasing shares of an investment trust or corporation. Your dollars are pooled with those of hundreds of other investors, and these combined monies are then invested and managed by professionals in large, diversified purchases of stocks, bonds, and various money market papers. This diversification helps insulate you against wide fluctuations in the prices of individual stocks. A professional does the buying and selling.

Mutual funds are open-ended—that is, like stocks, shares are continually available and they can be bought or sold at any time. The actual price of a fund is determined at the end of the day and is based upon the total value of securities in the fund's portfolio.

Choosing a Stock Mutual Fund

Before beginning your search for the right fund, you should know the difference between load and no-load funds. Load funds, sold by stockbrokers and mutual fund salesmen, are "loaded" with a sales charge or fee. Commissions for the purchase or sale of the fund generally range from about 4 percent to 8½ percent of the total price. Keep in mind that this means the value of the fund must escalate by that amount before you can break even. Although there is no difference in the performance of a load fund over a no-load fund, you might as well find one without a commission and save the difference for investing. But sometimes people like to buy load funds because they come recommended by their stockbroker; they find it easier to let him do the fund selection for them.

No-load funds have no sales commissions; you purchase shares directly from the fund itself, not through a stockbroker, and you pay only a small annual charge for administration and management. This ranges from 0.5 percent to 1.5 percent of the fund's total assets annually, as is true of load funds, too. For a complete list of no-load funds, write to:

No-Load Mutual Fund Association
11 Penn Plaza, Suite 2204
New York, NY 10001

or

The Investment Company Institute
1600 M Street N.W.
Washington, DC 20036

This institute also has a helpful guide called the *Mutual Fund Fact Book*, which is available for $2.00.

So, even if you go the route of a mutual fund, you're still not entirely free of decision making. Now you must, of course, decide which fund you want—there are over 1,200 to chose from! You can narrow your choice, however, by following these steps.

Step 1:
Clarify Your Goals.

Do you want a fund for income or for growth? Do you want a fund that consists primarily of stocks, bonds, or some of each? Do you want a high-risk speculative fund, or a more conservative one? Each fund has different investment objectives, so it is important that you understand these differences before making your selection. The fund's objectives are noted at the beginning of the prospectus, which is the official description of the fund required by the Securities and Exchange Commission. For example, a prospectus might read: "Our primary objective is safety of principal and long-term growth through the purchase of high-quality stocks in growth areas of the economy."

Step 2:
Study the Types of Funds.

Funds fall into several broad categories. Because of the boom in mutual funds over the past few years, you can select today from a broad range. There are funds that emphasize growth, others that focus on income. Some have tax-free holdings, others aim at capital appreciation or have speculative holdings. In selecting a fund, be realistic about how much time you can afford to spend watching it go up and down. The more speculative its portfolio, the more you need to keep your eye on it in order to know when to get out when its value starts to fall.

Here are the basic types of stock funds.

- **Growth Funds**. These seek long-term capital appreciation by buying stocks in companies that will grow faster than the rate of inflation. Dividend payments are usually low.

  Within this category there are the following:

  (1) **Aggressive or speculative funds**. These also seek maximum profit, but at a fast rate which is often achieved by taking greater risks, by selling short, or even by borrowing money for additional leverage. These are also known as maximum capital gains funds.

  (2) **Industry funds**. These specialize in one type of stock, such as energy stocks.

- **Income Funds**. These invest primarily in corporate bonds and are not concerned with growth. Some invest in high-dividend stocks. For more on bond income funds, see pages 66–68.

- **Growth and Income Funds**. Also called "balanced funds," these maintain portfolios that combine stocks and bonds and emphasize low risk. These portfolios often consist of leading companies that pay high dividends.

- **Municipal Bond Funds**. These are designed for tax-exempt income. (See page 68)

- **Money Market Funds**. (See pages 42–49)

- **Specialized Funds**. We will not discuss these funds, for they tend to be very speculative in nature and are not generally appropriate for the $5,000 investor. If you are interested in any of them, your broker can help you find the best. They include option funds, hedge funds, venture capital funds, gold funds, and so forth.

Step 3:
Study Management's
Performance Record.

Rating services publish the performance records of mutual funds over various time periods. These appear in several financial publications including *Barron's* and *Money* magazine. In addition, consult these and other publications at your library or broker's office:

- *Investment Companies* by The Wiesenberger Investment Companies Service. Published annually, this reference book has over 700 pages and covers nearly every existing fund. Cost $245

- *Johnson's Charts* covers 620 funds and shows what happens to a $10,000 investment over ten years in a number of different funds. Cost: $215

- *Donoghue's Mutual Funds Almanac* describes 850 funds and their ten-year performance records. Cost: $23

Once you have decided what type of fund you want, follow these easy tips in making your final selection.

- Find a fund that has at least $100 million in assets. If a fund is too small it may not be able to pay for first-rate analysts and a research staff. An exception to this rule is a small fund that is part of an umbrella organization, which is also known as a family of funds.

- Check the fund's annual performance rating in the sources listed on page 49.

- Find out from the fund's prospectus how long the fund has been in existence. Don't select one that has not had enough time to post a track record.

- Look for a fund that is increasing in size, not decreasing.

- Select a fund that is part of a family of funds and has switching privileges (more on switching below).

All in the Family

Even after you have selected a fund, you may be nervous about how it will react to sudden changes in the economy, in interest rates, or the market. One way to resolve this dilemma is to keep your money in a family of funds that offers more than one type of fund under the same corporate roof. You should look for a fund family that has a bond fund, a stock fund, and a money market fund so that you can switch your money from one fund to another as the economic climate changes. Pick a fund in which switching is free of charge or offered at a very nominal amount. The prospectus will tell you if you are limited to a certain number of switches per year. Make certain, too, that you can do your switching over the telephone.

How do you know when to switch? It requires time and study, but in general:

- When interest rates fall, keep your money in a mutual fund that has a stock portfolio.

- When interest rates rise, switch to a money market fund.

- When you see the price of the equities held in your fund going down, switch to a money market fund.

Through a family of funds you can take advantage of surges in prices and fluctuations in interest rates. There are about sixty fund families on the market today, and they offer more than three hundred individual funds. The largest are Fidelity with twenty-six funds and Vanguard with twenty-two. No one fund should be regarded as economically viable for all times. The market is cyclical, constantly changing, so never make an investment and think that's it. You must continually monitor all investments, including mutual funds.

If you feel ready to try switching among a family of funds, you may want to examine one of the newsletters that advises readers on how and when to move among the various mutual funds. This list is not a recommendation, only a guide to what is available.

Telephone Switch Newsletter
P.O. Box 2583
Huntington Beach, CA 92647
monthly; $97/year.

Switch Fund Advisory
Schabacker Investment Management
8943 Shady Grove Court
Gaithersburg, MD 20877
monthly; $105/year

Other mutual fund newsletters include:

Growth Fund Guide
Growth Fund Research Building
Eureka, CA 96097
13 issues per year; $76

The No-Load Fund Investor
P.O. Box 283
Hastings-on-Hudson, NY 10706
four issues per year; $24

No-Load Fund X
235 Montgomery Street
San Francisco, CA 94104
monthly; $77/year

Most mutual funds allow you to switch by telephone. Some limit the number of times you can switch, others do not. Check the box on the fund's application indicating your wish to switch and ask for the prospectus of every fund within the family. By law, you cannot buy or switch without having received a prospectus.

The fund will tape-record your order, your name, and account number. You will be asked whether or not you received the prospectus. Before you call, write down how many shares or how much money you want to transfer and the funds you are transferring from and to. Make you own notes on the transaction, including the name of the person who takes your order.

Leading performers over the past several years among the family of funds have been:

Kemper
120 South LaSalle Street
Chicago, IL 60603

Value Line
711 Third Avenue
New York, NY 10017

Oppenheimer
2 Broadway
New York, NY 10004

Fidelity
82 Devonshire Street
Boston, MA 02109

Regardless of the type of mutual fund you select—whether it is speculative in nature or devoted to income, growth, or tax-free returns—you must monitor its performance. Review your return once every four to six months. It's tempting to let the experts do the work, and for the most part you can. But experts can be wrong, economic conditions can change, and some funds can and do do better than others. So, keep track of your fund's returns, and when you see it slipping, give serious consideration to changing.

PART FIVE

The First $2,500

14 Bank MMDAs

Top-notch protection *and* liquidity. This almost unbeatable combination is available when you open a **money market deposit account (MMDA)** at your bank. Authorized on December 14, 1982, these accounts are insured for up to $100,000 and also pay money market rates without locking up your money for any given period. They are, in fact, an insured variation of the regular money market mutual fund.

Rules and Regulations

According to federal law, you originally needed a minimum balance of $2,500 to open and maintain a MMDA; but in 1985, this minimum is $1,000 and by 1986 there will be no legal minimum deposit at all. At that point, minimum amounts will be determined by individual banks.

Keep in mind that both yields and penalties imposed for falling below the minimum vary widely from bank to bank. Once again, it pays to shop around—some banks let you transfer funds to an ordinary checking account by telephone or ATM (automatic teller machine).

With a bank money market deposit account, you can write only three checks per month (to a third party) against your balance, although you are allowed to withdraw money in person as often as you like—as long as you keep your minimum balance. Usually there is no minimum amount on the size of the checks.

The interest rate on these accounts is generally, but not always, half a percentage point below that of Treasury bills. Banks adjust the rate periodically along with changes in short-term interest rates. Of course, they tend to remain competitive with the money market mutual fund rates. Both, after all, are aggressively going after your savings dollars.

There is a key difference in the way in which interest is paid to depositors of money market deposit accounts and to shareholders in a money market mutual fund. Money market mutual funds *must* pay out most of their earnings to the fund's shareholders.* Although banks are not required to pay out all that they earn, they are obliged by law to post the interest rate they will pay each month. Although banks can pay whatever rate they want, in general you can expect bank rates to be slightly lower, since the money is insured. On the whole, the difference between bank money market deposit accounts and money market mutual funds is usually negligible.

If you're an active investor or a saver who tends to move money around a lot, this multipurpose account could be extremely useful. You get immediate access to your money and it allows you to use other bank services as well.

Because terms and rates do vary so from bank to bank, as well as from region to region, nationwide shopping for MMDAs has become an important investment trend. And, not surprisingly, several publications have sprung into existence to help you find the best rates, which could turn out to be anywhere from Kansas City to Des Moines to Lake Charles.

A percentage is retained to cover the cost of operating the fund.

For help on money market rates and CD rates, you can consult:

> *100 Highest Yields*
> Advertising News Service, Inc.
> P.O. Box 402608
> Miami Beach, FL 33140
> 305-531-0037
> Weekly: $89/year; $49/6 months
> Lists the top yields nationwide on five federally insured bank and thrift investment products
>
> *Bank Rate Monitor*
> Advertising News Service, Inc.
> P.O. Box 402608
> Miami Beach, FL 33140
> 305-531-0037
> Weekly: $245/year
> Gives the rates, averages, and pricing on MMDAs and CDs; includes a national index
>
> *Money Fund Safety Ratings*
> The Institute for Econometric Research
> 3471 North Federal Highway
> Fort Lauderdale, FL 33306
> 800-327-6720; 305-536-9000
> Monthly: $49/year
> Rates the money funds nationwide
>
> *Savers Rate News*
> Savers Advisory Service, Inc.
> P.O. Box 143520
> Coral Gables, FL 33114
> 800-327-0331; 305-751-7521
> Biweekly: $25/year.
> Special rate for citizens over age 65: $15/year
> Provides updates on latest high yields on various CDs

Money Market Mutual Fund

- Best for those who switch from bonds to stocks to money market funds
- Best for those who dip into their funds often
- You can write as many checks as you like ($150 or $500 minimum per check is common).
- No service charges
- Not insured (except for a very few funds

Bank Money Market Deposit Account

- Best for savers
- Best for those who do not dip into their money very often
- You can write only three checks per month to third parties.
- You can withdraw money in person as often as you like.
- Insured up to $100,000
- Service charges
- Penalties for dropped below minimum balance

BANK MONEY MARKET DEPOSIT ACCOUNTS

For Whom

- Investors who know they can maintain the minimum balance
- Those who want high market rates and instant liquidity
- Those seeking a safe parking place for their savings or emergency money

Minimum

- $1,000 minimum balance in 1985; no legal minimum in 1986 (to be determined by individual banks)

Safety Factor

- Very high
- Insured up to $100,000

Advantages

- High interest rates
- You can transfer money to checking account (three preauthorized transfers per month).
- You can withdraw in person as often as you like.
- You can get money out easily if interest rates drop.

Disadvantages

- Some banks have penalties for withdrawl.
- You must maintain a minimum balance (until scheduled change in regulations).
- You can write only three checks per month.
- If balance falls below minimum, interest rate may revert back to passbook rate.
- If balance falls below minimum, some banks will pay no interest at all.
- If balance falls below minimum, some banks impose a monthly charge and may or may not pay interest.

Special Hints

- Find a bank money market deposit account that can be linked electronically to your NOW or SuperNow account and to the bank's automatic teller machine network. Then you can write more than the three minimum checks since there is no limit on how often you can personally make transfers. In other words, if the accounts are connected, you can keep most of your money in the high paying MMDA and transfer funds into your checking account only as you need to.

- Select a bank that allows you to connect your MMDA to a brokerage account so you can buy stocks, bonds, and Treasuries via telephone.

- Look at the effective annual yield. That is easier to compare than deciphering each different bank's compounding methods.

- Find out if your interest rate will be lowered to passbook rate if your account falls below the required minimum. Find a bank that cuts the rate only for the days when your balance is below the minimum, not one that penalizes you for the entire week or month.

15 SuperNOW Bank Accounts

Unlimited check-writing privileges and above-average interest are yours in a SuperNOW account, another consideration for the investor who has $2,500 and needs an interest-bearing checking account.

The **SuperNOW** is a hybrid bank account combining the advantages of the NOW account (see Chapter 8) and a money market account (see Chapter 9). Plus—it is insured for up to $100,000.

SuperNOWs pay high interest rates, which are always above the 5.25 percent legal maximum rate on ordinary NOW accounts but usually below money market fund accounts. In fact, SuperNOWs can pay whatever rate the bank determines. The plan also comes with unlimited check-writing privileges.

In order to earn high rates, it is mandatory that you maintain the prescribed minimum balance of $2,500. Otherwise, by law, the interest rate will fall to 5.25 percent. In addition, many banks slap on extra fees, ranging from $5 to $15 per month.

Launched on January 5, 1983, these interest-bearing checking accounts have drawn mixed reviews. In general, interest rates are no longer as spectacular as when SuperNOWs first came on the scene. They tend to be higher, of course, than the NOW rate, but less than the money market deposit account rate. (And as you recall, the NOW account minimum balance requirement is significantly lower.)

On the other hand, bank money market deposit accounts, which have a minimum investment requirement but limited check-writing privileges, are paying higher rates. The reason for the lower SuperNOW rates is that checking accounts are expensive for banks to run. Consequently, many banks also add service charges and checking fees to additionally offset these costs. This naturally reduces the effective yield on what you get through a SuperNOW account.

Another drawback to consider is that the interest earned in this type of account is fully taxable as income.

Go for a SuperNOW *only* if you find a bank that is paying as much as the average money market deposit account and also offers free or very low cost checking. (Some banks charge as much as 35 cents per check.)

Otherwise, one of the other options described in this book is probably a better bet for you. For example, look for a money market deposit account or a money market mutual fund combined with a low-cost, basic checking account, and transfer money from the fund into your checking account as you need it to cover checks.

SUPERNOW ACCOUNTS

For Whom

- Those who want to write a lot of checks and receive more interest than the 5.25 percent paid in a NOW account

Fee or Minimum

- Must maintain a balance of $2,500
- May be charged for individual checks
- May be charged a monthly fee

Safety Factor

- Insured up to $100,000
- High

Advantages

- Idle money can earn high interest here
- Unlimited check writing privileges

Disadvantages

- Interest rate drops to 5.25 percent if balance falls below $2,500
- May be extra penalties when balance is below minimum

THE 72 RULE

A quick way to calculate how long it will take you to double your investment—at any interest rate—is to use "The 72 Rule."

Divide 72 by the interest rate and you get the number of years it will take to double your money.

For example: 72 divided by 9½ percent is 7.6 years
72 divided by 11 percent is 6½ years

Note: "The 72 rule" applies only when interest and dividends are reinvested. It does not take taxes into consideration.

16 Public Utilities

P ublic utility companies have traditionally been sound, high-yielding investments and as such are considered safe enough for "widows and orphans." Because of their return and high safety ranking, you can invest at the $1,000 level, even though other common stocks are better purchased with investments of $5,000 or more. In general, of course, the greater the risk element in an investment, the more money you should have to cushion any losses.

Public utilities are corporations with special licenses, called "certificates of public convenience and necessity," which allow them to operate and sell electric power and natural gas in a designated geographical area. This license gives the company a monopoly within its service area. Rates charged to customers for gas or electricity are controlled by state public utility commissions.

Divident Reinvestment Plans

And, public utilities offer a plus that other stocks don't—a special tax shelter that you should take advantage of. Of course when you buy stocks in most corporations, your dividends are taxed as income; but investors who own shares of common stock in *some* public utility gas and electric companies may put off paying taxes on their dividends until they sell their stocks.

In order to benefit from this tax ruling, however, you must participate in a qualified Dividend Reinvestment Plan (DRP). In other words, your dividends must be plowed back into the company immediately. For example, if Company ABC declares an annual dividend of $2 on a stock selling for $20 per share, the investor who elects to take cash will receive $2 for each share he owns in four quarterly payments. Those, however, who opt for a DRP will receive fractional shares of stock each quarter, ultimately equaling one new share for each ten shares owned.

The total amount you can shelter from the Internal Revenue Service through a DRP is $750 per year for an individual and $1,500 for a married couple filing a joint income tax return. This tax break is scheduled to end December 31, 1985; however, there is pressure on Congress to extend it. Your stockbroker can give you the current list of utility companies that participate in DRP as well as information on the likelihood that the ruling will be extended.

Other Advantages

There are three other potential advantages available when you buy common stock in public utility companies:

1. Some utilities tag on an added bonus: a 5 percent discount on the stock purchase price when shares are bought through the dividend reinvestment program.

2. Some utilities declare all or part of their dividends—on an annual basis—as a "return of capital." This means the dividends are exempt from federal and, in some cases, state and local taxes.

3. When you hold your stock for six months or more, the profit on the accumulated dividends receives preferential capital gains treatment. That means a maximum federal tax of only 20 percent.

The triple benefits—tax deferral, discount purchase price, and capital gains treatment of dividends—when combined with high safety and yields make most of these stocks suitable for even the most conservative investor. Like any common stock, however, they fluctuate in price, sometimes dramatically so. Thus *they are not entirely risk free.*

In addition, during the last two decades, many public utilities have undertaken gigantic projects to produce electricity from nuclear power. Yet, because of the mounting public concern surrounding nuclear energy, some of these projects have been canceled or postponed with serious financial consequences for the sponsoring utility company. Your stockbroker will be able to help you determine which utilities are free of this uncertainty. You can also check the ratings listed in *Standard & Poor's* and *Value Line.*

PART SIX

When You Have $5,000

17 Stocks: Growth & Income

Almost everyone at some point in his or her life entertains the idea of buying a stock, a piece of American industry. Many actually do more than just think about it—over 14 percent of the U.S. population owns stocks (that's about 32.6 million Americans).

According to a recent study done by the New York Stock Exchange, individual investors buy and sell an average of 25 million shares a day.

There are four compelling reasons why, at the $5,000 level, you, too, should consider buying stocks:

- Over the long term, stocks tend to outperform bonds.

- Stocks offer the possibility of appreciation.

- Stocks offer the possibility of keeping ahead of inflation.

- Gains on stocks, if held long term, are taxed at the lower, more favorable capital gains rate.

Are You Ready for the Market?

Prior to selecting stocks for your own portfolio, you must have money set aside for an emergency. At least three months' worth of living expenses should be safely stashed away in a liquid investment, such as a money market mutual fund, a money market deposit account, or a certificate of deposit (see pages 42–56). Once this has been accomplished and you have accumulated $5,000, you're ready to go. (Although it *is* possible to invest in the market with smaller amounts of money, in order to establish a truly diversified portfolio you need a base of about $5,000.)

First, *determine your investment goals*. Are you seeking a stock that pays a high cash dividend, or would you prefer to buy one that will appreciate substantially in price? Do you want liquidity—that is, the ability to get money back when you want it, or are you content to wait for long-term growth? Your goals make a difference, because no one stock offers high dividends, instant liquidity, spectacular appreciation, plus stability.

The Risk Factor

But, before you invest, keep in mind that while many stocks are profitable investments and return handsome rewards in terms of capital appreciation, they also can decline in price. *There is no guarantee that you will make a profit*. Careful selection is essential.

The ABCs of Stock Selection

When you have accumulated $5,000 *and* established an emergency nest egg, you can prudently consider investing either for growth or income through purchase of common stocks. A **common stock** is a fractional share of ownership in a corporation. For example, if a corporation has one million outstanding shares and you buy one share, you then own one-millionth of that corporation.

This ownership enables you to participate in the fortunes and growth of the corporation. If the corporation prospers, its earnings (which are expressed as earnings per share) will rise, which in turn tends to make the price of the stock rise. Simply put, the corporation's value has increased. Generally, some part of these earnings is shared with stockholders in the form of a cash dividend which is paid out four times a year.

If you believe that certain corporations or industries will flourish in the coming years, try selecting several common stocks in these areas as an investment for income, growth, or a combination of the two. As a general rule, don't put more than 10 percent of your funds into the stock of any one company and no more than 20 percent in any one industry.

Remember that stocks can also decline in price and you should try to confine your selections primarily to blue chip companies, that is, large, well-financed, and established corporations with secure positions within their industry.

Here are five key standards to use in judging a stock.

1. Earnings per share should show an upward trend over the last five years. If, however, earnings declined for one year out of five, this is acceptable, provided the overall trend continues to rise.

Earnings per share, simply defined, is the company's net income (after taxes and money for preferred stock dividends) divided by the average number of common stock shares outstanding. You will find it listed in the company's annual report or in professional materials such as *Value Line* or Standard & Poor's *Stock Guide*, available at your library or in any broker's office.

2. Increasing earnings should be accompanied by similarly increasing dividends. You should study the cash dividend payments over the last five-year period. In some cases a corporation will use most of its earnings to invest in future growth, and then dividends may be quite modest and rightly so. But even in these cases, some token dividend should be paid annually. Ideally, a company should earn at least $5 for every $4 it pays out.

In conjunction with the company's dividend, you should note its **yield** which is the current dividend divided by the price of a share. It is listed in the newspaper along with the dividend and other statistics. The yield should be higher in a stock you purchase for income than in one selected for potential price appreciation (see sample stock listing, page 106).

3. Standard & Poor's rates each company's financial strength. For you, the $5,000 investor, the minimum acceptable rating should be A—.

4. The number of outstanding shares should be at least ten million. Marketability and liquidity depend upon a large supply of common stock shares. Ten million shares ensures activity by the major institutions, such as mutual funds, pension funds, and insurance companies. Institutional participation helps guarantee an active market in which you and others can readily buy and sell the company's stock.

5. Study the company's price to earnings ratio (P/E ratio). This ratio is found by dividing the last year's earnings per share (or the current year's estimated earnings) into the current price of the stock. The **P/E ratio** is one of the most important analytical tools in the business. It reflects investor opinion about the stock and about the market as a whole. For example, a P/E of 11 means investors are willing to pay 11 times earnings for that stock. A P/E of 11 indicates greater investor interest and confidence than a P/E of 7 or 5, for example.

A P/E ratio under 10 is considered conservative and, depending upon the company, its industry, and your broker's advice, you can feel comfortable with a P/E of 10 or less. As a company's P/E moves above 10, you begin to pay a premium for some aspect of the company's future. For example, a P/E ratio above 10 may very well be justified by outstanding prospects for future growth, by new technological advances or by worldwide shortages of a product that the company produces.

Basically, the P/E ratio is the measure of the common stock's value to investors. A low P/E of 5 or 6 usually means that the prospects are clouded by uncertainty.

Similarly, a P/E of 14 or 15 indicates a keen appetite on the part of investors to participate in that company's future.

Whatever stock or stocks you decide to buy, you want to get in at the lowest possible P/E—before there is a lot of investor interest and the P/E is bid up. No one can say exactly what ratio you should accept, and it is here that your selection process and your broker's advice become important.

How to Read a Financial Page

Once you own stocks, you will want to know how they are doing —whether they are going up or down in price. To find out, you can read the market quotations in the daily newspaper.

You will find your stock listed under the name of its exchange —the New York Stock Exchange, American Stock Exchange, Over-the-Counter, and so forth. Here's how it works, using IBM— International Business Machines Corporation—as an example (prices are quoted in fractions of a dollar, so $126½ means $126.50 per share):

52 week High	Low	Stock	Div	Yield %	P/E ratio	Sales 100s	High	Low	Last	Chg
134¼	99	IBM	4.40	3.5	13	4477	127¾	126¼	126½	+³⁄₈

- The first two columns tell the highest and the lowest prices per share for the last 52 weeks. In the case of IBM, they are $134¼ and $99.

- The next column gives an abbreviated form of the stock's name. Here it is IBM.

- Then comes the annual dividend, if any. For IBM it is $4.40.

- Following the dividend is the stock's yield, which is given as a percentage. To determine the yield, divide the dividend by the closing price: $4.40 divided by $126.50 = 3.5%.

- After the yield comes the P/E ratio or price divided by earnings. You will note that earnings are not listed in the paper. The P/E here is 13.

- The number 4477 in the next column indicates the number of shares traded that particular day. It is listed in hundreds, so 447,700 shares of IBM were traded on that day.

- The next two numbers, $127¾ and $126¼ tell how high and how low the stock traded that day. In other words, during the course of the day, some stock traded as high as 127¾ and some trades were made for as little as 126¼ per share. The following column shows the price of the final trade that day, and the final column illustrates the change in the closing price from the prior day. In this case it was $126½ which was ³/₈ (or $.375) over the preceding day's closing price. Sometimes there will be a minus sign, indicating it fell in price. If there's no plus or minus sign, then the closing price was the same as the day before. *Note:* These figures do not include the broker's commission.

Buying Stocks

Once you have decided to become involved with the stock market, the next issue to resolve is whether to use a broker or to select your own stocks. Generally speaking, if you have never owned a stock before, it is probably more prudent to get help from an experienced professional than to go it alone.

Selecting a Broker

Knowing when and how to seek the advice of an expert is a critical part of being a successful investor. If you've never had a broker (or, if you've had one you did not like) you can find the right one by doing some investigative work well in advance. Plan on spending three to four weeks to locate the broker who is right for you.

Start by thinking about how you selected your doctor or lawyer. Someone else probably suggested them to you. Getting the recommendations of friends and colleagues whose judgment you respect is one of the best ways to find a good broker. Ask your boss, your banker, your uncle, or your pediatrician if they have a broker they like.

After gathering several names, call and make appointments with each one. Tell them the amount of money you have to invest. Not all brokers are interested in small accounts, yet many are. Those who are realize that a small account obviously has the potential of becoming a larger one over time. A number of the major "full service" houses, such as Merrill Lynch, Paine Webber, Shearson/American Express, E.F. Hutton, and Bache Halsey Stuart Shields, are indeed willing to open small accounts. Merrill Lynch has a special program for small investors, described on page 34. You will also find that reliable regional brokers are set up to handle accounts of all sizes, and they are eager to help local investors. If you feel you don't need investment advice, you can save on commissions by buying through a "discount" broker, such as Charles Schwab. In either event, a broker must execute the final buy or sell transaction for you.

Before you interview your broker candidates, prepare a list of questions to ask them. It should include these four items, plus anything else that conerns you:

1. *Do you handle accounts of this size?* You certainly don't want to use a broker who is uninterested in $5,000.

2. *Can you give me one or two references?* Avoid any broker who says no.

3. *How long have you been a broker?* Any broker tends to look good in a good market. You want an experienced person who knows how to handle money in bad times as well as good.

4. *How should I invest my $5,000?* Beware of the broker who advises you to put it all in one stock, or even all in the market. Unless you have specifically said the total amount is to be invested in stocks, the broker should advise you to diversify.

For additional details on how to select a broker you may want to read: *How to Talk to a Broker* by Jay J. Pack. New York: Harper & Row 1985.

Going It Alone

Once you have gained some feeling for the market, you may want to plunge right in and do your own stock selection. If you decide to follow this course, you must be prepared to regard it as a learning experience, for *it is very unlikely you will pick all winners*—even the pros don't manage to do that. So, at first, avoid putting more money than you can afford to lose in the market.

The best way to minimize your risks, of course, is to be well informed. To be your own broker you must be prepared to spend a significant amount of time reading about the economy and about individual companies, as well as the major industries.

WHERE YOU CAN FIND INFORMATION

1. *The New York Stock Exchange* (Dept. of Public Information, 11 Wall Street, New York, NY 10005) has a free list of member firms with the minimum amount required to open an account provided along with addresses and telephone numbers. Write also for a list of their low-cost pamphlets on investing. One of the most useful ones is: *Income Leaders on the Big Board*, which contains stocks and bonds listed on the NYSE that yield 8 percent or more and meet specified quality standards. The stocks included meet the following criteria:
   —dividends paid in each of the past five years
   —earnings in each of the past five years
   —increase in earnings per share from 1974 on.

2. *Specialized financial periodicals and newspapers* are excellent sources of information on the general economic climate and the stock market. In particular: *Barron's*, *The Wall Street Journal*, *The New York Times*, *Financial News Daily*, and *The Chicago Tribune* among the newspapers. Good magazines are: *Forbes*, *Business Week*, *Financial World*, *Fortune*, *U.S. News*, and *Fact*. We have mentioned previously *Better Investing*, the monthly magazine of the National Association of Investment Clubs. Devoted to investment educa-

tion, it analyzes stocks and covers various views on investments (see page 37).

3. *Brokerage firms have a wealth of research material.* The large houses will send you some material, even if you are not a customer —at least for a limited period. Many have copies of newsletters on display in their retail offices. Although much of this information is generally known, you can still gather ideas, and certainly it is valuable for background data.

4. *Annual reports of corporations are an important source.* Write or call any company you are considering investing in for a copy and then read the section on How to Read an Annual Report (pages 121–24).

5. *Standard & Poor's New York Stock Exchange Reports,* a large loose-leaf volume, is regarded as a bible in the financial world. It contains one page, both sides, on each company listed on the NYSE. S&P also publishes similar volumes for the American Stock Exchange and for over-the-counter stocks. The material is revised periodically. For each corporation you will find: a summary description, the current outlook, and new developments, plus a ten-year statistical table.

6. *Standard & Poor's Stock Guide* is a small monthly booklet containing basic data in condensed form on 5,000 stocks: price range, P/E ratio, dividend history, sales, an abbreviated balance sheet, earnings, and the S&P rating. A similar monthly booklet is put out covering bonds. For further details on all S&P publications, write to:

Standard and Poor's Corporation
25 Broadway
New York, NY 10004

7. *Value Line Investment Survey* contains the most comprehensive coverage of stocks. Value Line follows 1,700 companies and their industries. Each industry is updated quarterly. Stocks are ranked on the basis of timeliness for purchase and safety. A subscription to this service also includes a separate weekly analysis of the market and general economic situation plus an in-depth discussion of one stock recommended for purchase.

8. *Financial newsletters can be helpful, but they vary enormously in reliability and success as far as their advice goes.* Before subscribing to any newsletter, try to locate copies at your library or by contacting the publisher. Many will send a fee copy or offer trial subscriptions at a reduced rate.

There is also a service that rates the advisors. *Hulbert Financial Digest* is a monthly newsletter that tracks and ranks fifty of the stock market newsletters based on their performance in recommending stocks. One issue costs $5; a five-month subscription is $33.75; a full year's subscription is $135. Contact: Hulbert Financial Digest, 409 First Street S.E., Washington, DC 20003; 202-546-2164.

9. *Sale and purchase of a company's stock by officials of the corporation is one way to determine trends in the price of the stock.* There are a number of newsletters that chart the so-called insider trading. If copies are unavailable at your public library or broker's office, write to the publisher and ask for a free sample and information about trial subscriptions. This listing is in no way a recommendation.

Consensus of Insiders. Perry Wysong Publications. P.O. Box 10247, Fort Lauderdale, FL 33334; weekly; $247/year

The Insiders. Norman Fosback, editor. 3471 North Federal Highway, Fort Lauderdale, FL 33306; semi-monthly; $49/year

The Insiders' Chronicle. William Mehlman, editor. P.O. Box 9662, Arlington, VA 22209; 50 issues per year; $325/year

Insiders Edge Highlights Report. Richard A. Horowitz, editor. 122 Spanish Village, Suite 644; Dallas, TX 75248; monthly; $79/year

YOUR INVESTMENT ACHILLES HEEL

Even with rational research and thoughtful planning on your part, you may still fall prey to one or more of the ubiquitous emotional traps that lie in wait in the investment field.

Every investor has areas of vulnerability. If you recognize yours, it's then possible to eliminate many errors and reduce misjudgments. Here are the five most common pitfalls small investors make when buying and selling stocks.

1. Tendency to hold on to securities too long, hoping a poor performer will turn around

2. Reacting immediately to bad news and selling too soon

3. Refusing to sell and take the profit because you feel you can squeeze out a few more points

4. Refusing to take a profit because of capital gains tax, even when the stock is fully valued

5. Avoiding selling a stock you inherited because of sentimental feelings

One way to avoid these and other pitfalls is to have a game plan, to know what your financial objectives are and then stick to them.

Save Twice with DRPs

If you already own stock in a company that has a dividend reinvestment plan (DRP), you can bypass a stockbroker and have your dividends reinvested automatically in order to buy more of that firm's common stock in your name. There are two key advantages to participating in a DRP whenever possible: 1) you obviously eliminate the broker's fees or commissions for buying the stock; and 2) you save the cash or dividend money you might otherwise spend. Nationwide close to 200 companies will turn your dividends into stocks at a discount from the current market price. This discount DRP offers the most economical way to build a portfolio.

Although utility companies (see Chapter 16) and banks constitute the majority of the companies with discount DRPs, there are many other participating industries. Most companies are extremely solid and have a long history of continual dividend payments to their shareholders.

No two companies have exactly the same DRP—each one has its own variation on the theme and, upon written request, will send you a descriptive brochure on how to participate. In order to get started, you must already own one share of common stock in a given company. Generally, the company requires that the stock be registered in your name, not in the street name (i.e., the name of the broker's firm).

Once you sign up for the DRP, the company no longer pays you a cash dividend but instead sends the money to its DRP agent, usually a bank, to be invested along with any optional cash investment you may have sent in. This money then goes to purchase shares, or, if you don't have enough money for a full share, a partial share, of the company's stock. Most DRPs have three investment choices. You can:

1. Automatically invest all your dividends every quarter and purchase shares of common stock at a discount,

2. Have a part of your dividend sent to you in cash and a part of it reinvested, or

3. Make optional cash investments in addition to reinvesting your dividends. Many companies limit optional cash investments to $3,000 to $5,000 per quarter. Some companies actually require a small additional cash investment ranging from $10 to $30.

SEVEN STOCK MARKET DO'S

- Know whether you're investing for long-term appreciation or immediate income, and select stocks that match your goal.

- If you're investing long term, remember that the market fluctuates daily and the item to focus on is earnings, not price.

- Know about the industry. Don't purchase a medical technology stock or a high-tech issue without first studying the industry.

- Read the company's annual and quarterly reports before buying.

- Stick with companies that are leaders within their industry.

- Look for companies with a proven record of consistant growth.

- Be patient.

- Don't think you will get rich overnight. Looking for instant gratification is a common mistake new investors make.

- Don't buy a stock merely because someone gave you a so-called "hot tip." Check the facts first.

- Don't rush out to sell a winning stock while holding on to a loser.

- Don't fall in love with your stocks.

- Don't wait to buy until everyone likes a stock or until there's only good news. By then it will have run up in price.

- Don't buy companies heavily burdened by debt.

- Don't hesitate to cut your losses.

18 Margin Accounts

Believe it or not, when you buy stocks you do *not* always have to pay the full purchase price. Quick credit is available from your brokerage firm through what is called a **margin account**. Buying on margin simply means buying on credit, and it's not as complicated as it sounds. You put up part of the purchase price and borrow the rest from your broker at a specified interest rate.

How Does It Work?

If you had $2,000 to invest in a stock selling at $10 per share, you could buy 200 shares if you paid the full purchase price of $2,000. But, if you bought on margin, you could borrow $2,000 from your broker, put up $2,000 yourself, and buy 400 shares.

Why would investors with $5,000 want to use this creditable way to buy stocks and bonds?

- The interest they pay to the broker is tax deductible.

- They might want to buy more stock than they have ready cash for.

- The interest rate they could receive on certain bonds is sometimes higher than the margin interest rate they would pay to borrow the money to buy those bonds.

- They might want to speculate without laying out too much cash.

- They might have a more pressing temporary need for their available cash but don't want to pass up a good investment opportunity.

Before you open a margin account you should be aware of the risks involved.

1. The difference between your margin loan and the market value of stocks and bonds in your account must be a minimum of 25 percent. If the value of your securities falls so that the equity in the account is below 25 percent, you may get a "margin call," in which case you must add cash or securities to your account and bring the equity back up to 25 percent. For example:
- —200 shares of General Motors at $75/share = market value of $15,000
- —Original margin loan: $7,500
- —General Motors drops to $45/share
- —Your market value is now only $9,000 and your loan is still $7,500; the difference between the two is $1,500
- —To determine what percentage $1,500 is of $9,000, divide $1,500 by $9,000 to get 16.6 percent

—You are below 25 percent and therefore must bring up
   your account to $2,550, which is 25 percent of $9,000.

2. If you cannot provide enough cash or securities to bring your
equity back up to 25 percent, the broker is obliged to sell enough
securities from your account to meet the 25 percent minimum.

3. Interest rates on margin loans may rise.

Any stock purchased on margin must be left with your broker
and it must be registered to you in the name of the brokerage
house. This is called registration "in the street name." The broker
may then pledge your stock as collateral for the firm's bank loan in
order to carry other margin accounts. If this should happen, the
stock is still yours and you still collect the dividends.

How much can you borrow on a margin loan? The Federal Reserve Board sets the minimum margin requirements: You can borrow 50 percent of the value of a stock (if it is listed on one of the exchanges or if it is designated marginable and traded over the count-
er), 70 percent of the value of a corporate bond, and 90 percent of
a U.S. Government bond. You must have $2,000 in cash or $4,000
in marketable securities in order to set up a margin account.

The margin interest rate (the interest rate you will be charged)
is generally based on the "broker call rate," which is the interest
rate that banks charge brokers when they borrow for short-term
periods. Brokers then add on an additional ½ percent or more
when they lend the money to you on margin. Rates vary from
broker to broker, so it pays to shop around.

Should You Try
a Margin Account?

Buying on margin or borrowing money on securities is not generally recommended for small or inexperienced investors, yet it may
be quite appropriate in some cases. If you have accumulated an extra $5,000 and are ready to become a serious investor, this is one
way to build up your portfolio. It is also suitable for investors with
low cash reserves and for people who need to raise cash quickly.

19 Options

You have probably heard this term and wondered if it applies to you. It may if you have $5,000 to invest in the stock market and you like to speculate.

An **option** represents the *right* to buy or sell a specific stock at a specified price (called the **strike price**), but only for a limited time. When you buy the option, you actually buy the right to buy the stock at the specified price. You do not need to own stocks to participate in options. If the stock price rises, the option price should rise with it, providing a profit if you sell your option. If the stock price falls, the option price also falls, and you will have a loss.

Calls and Puts

There are two kinds of options: **calls** and **puts**. Let's examine calls first. A call is the right to buy one hundred shares of a stock at a certain price for a certain time, usually three to nine months. Option prices are quoted daily in the newspaper, and they fluctuate even more widely than the prices of the underlying stock.

Here's how it works: Let's say you want to buy one hundred shares* of General Motors, which is selling at $75 per share. There are three ways you can do this:

1. You can spend $7,500 and pay cash for the 100 shares.

2. You can spend $3,750 and buy the 100 shares on margin (see pages 114–116).

3. You can spend $400, for example, and buy a call on General Motors.

**Options are always sold in units of 100.*

If you select choice number three, with the price of GM at $75 per share, you could, for example, pay $4 a share for the right to buy GM at $75 anytime during the next three months—regardless of any changes in the current market value of GM. So, if the stock goes up to $85 per share within those three months, your option will be worth $1,000 ($10 profit on 100 shares). You may then elect to sell the option for this $1,000 (less commissions) and realize a net profit of nearly $600. Here's the arithmetic:

$$\begin{array}{rl} \$85 & \text{price to which GM rises during 3 months} \\ -\ 75 & \text{price of GM strike option} \\ \hline 10 & \text{value of your option} \\ -\ 4 & \text{cost of your option} \\ \hline 6 & \times\ 100\ \text{shares} = \$600\ \text{profit.} \end{array}$$

In other words, you have profited by the 10-point rise in GM stock —without having actually bought and sold the stock. The option you bought and sold did it for you.

Should You Buy Calls?

Maybe...It's a highly risky business, so buy them *only* if you believe that a stock will increase in price by a large amount within a short time. If your judgment turns out to be correct, you will make a substantial gain on your speculation, 150 percent in the example of General Motors. But, if you are wrong, your loss could be as much as 100 percent.

Keep in mind that, in addition to the cost of your call (in this case it was $4 per share, or $400), you do not receive dividends when you own calls as you do when you own the actual stock. By and large, options are for those who like to speculate. This type of investor craves fast action with small amounts of money and has a large appetite for risk.

The second type of option is known as a put. It is an option to sell a stock at a specified price, the strike price, for a limited time. Let's use the same example with General Motors selling at $75. If you expect its price to fall substantially, then for $3 per share, for example, you can buy the right to sell, or "put," 100 shares at $75 for three months.

If the stock drops to $65 per share within this three-month period, you can make a $700 profit. Here's the arithmetic:

$$
\begin{array}{rl}
\$75 & \text{the price of exercise GM option} \\
-\ 65 & \text{price to which GM fell during 3 months} \\
\hline
10 & \text{value of your option} \\
-\ 3 & \text{cost of your option} \\
\hline
7 & \times\ 100\ \text{shares} = \$700\ \text{profit.}
\end{array}
$$

Should You Buy Puts?

Yes, if you believe a stock will have a substantial drop in price in a short time. If your hunch is right you can make a big percentage gain, as shown above. If you are wrong, your loss may be total.

As with buying calls, speculators are the most qualified to buy puts.

Reading the Option Tables

Option & closing price	Strike Price	Calls			Puts		
		Sept	Dec	Mar	Sept	Dec	Mar
Gen Motors							
75	65	10⅛	10⅞	11	¹⁄₁₆	¾	1½
75	70	5⅛	7¼	8	¼	1½	3¼
75	75	1	4	5	1	3	4½
75	80	¼	1¾	2¾	6	8	9

The first column gives the name of the stock and the current price —General Motors selling at $75 per share. Column two lists the different strike prices. The next three columns are the call prices for the different months of expiration. The last three columns give the put prices for the three months of expiration.

Expiration always occurs on the third Saturday of each month. In the General Motors table, the September options have less than two weeks to run since this example is dated September 14, 1984.

For instance, the option to buy GM at $75 per share was selling at $1 per share for the period ending in one week and one day; for $4 for the period ending on the third Saturday of December; and for $5 for the period ending on the third Saturday in March. (Naturally, you pay more for an option that is longer-lived.) Other options are similarly listed.

TIPS ON OPTIONS

- Invest a small amount in options if you are a beginner.

- Set specific profit-and-loss targets and take the profit as soon as the stock hits your target goal.

- Watch the price of the stock and your option every day. You must be prepared to have your broker sell you out fast.

- If your option is doing poorly, don't wait until the expiration date to sell; last-minute reversals are unlikely.

- If your broker suggests an option, ask him to explain exactly why and at what target point he would get you out. Not every broker is adept at handling options. Avoid one who does not give specific answers to your questions.

Appendix

"Dear Shareholder"

How to Read an Annual Report

Just looking at the pictures and skimming the headlines in an annual report won't really help you evaluate the investment potential of a company, but armed with a little knowledge ahead of time, you can glean a lot of useful material from even the thinnest report.

The typical annual report consists of a letter to the stockholders from the president or chairman, a description of the company's business operations, detailed financial tables, a mass of footnotes, and a statement by an outside auditor.

It's quite easy to get lost in this forest of financial statistics, yet by developing your own search system—one that can be used with any annual report—you will soon have a basic comprehension of the business you may wish to invest in.

A word of caution: Don't let slick, glossy paper, artistic photographs, and two-tier pullouts impress you unduly. These can be merely the work of a good public relations firm and not a true measure of the company. A simple presentation of the facts and an open divulging of financial statistics are what counts.

Step One

With an annual report, it's best to start at the back and review the material presented by the auditor-certified public accountant. This generally consists of a brief statement to the effect that the financial material was prepared in accordance with "generally accepted accounting principles" (GAAP). If that's it, then the company has been given a clean bill of health. If, however, the auditor's statement contains hedge clauses such as "the results are subject to," then beware. That's accountant-eze for an unresolved problem, perhaps a legal action that carries serious financial implications for the company. Frequently it implies that a ruling against the firm may lead to lower earnings than those printed in the annual report.

Some statements are even less subtle: "Uncertainties exist as to the corporation's ability to achieve future profitable operations." All auditor's reservations should be noted before reading.

Step Two

At the beginning of nearly every annual report is the president's or chairman's letter to the stockholders. Traditionally this is management's chance to comment on last year's results and the outlook for the future. It also reflects the tone and direction of the company as viewed by management. Yet you should be aware of hidden caveats here, too: "All development went along as expected except for..." or, "We will meet our stated goals on target unless..." These are red warning signals. Approach the statement from management as an opportunity to learn how they think and plan.

Step Three

Footnotes come next. They often define terms and conditions actually used in the financial pages, such as a change in accounting methods. The footnotes will also alert you to the fact that earnings are up because of a windfall that won't occur again next year, or that legal action is pending.

Step Four

After you've waded through the footnotes, turn to the income statement, usually located in the middle of the report. It will give you a good idea of what direction sales and earnings took during the year as compared with the previous year. If both earnings and sales went up during the year, it certainly is good news. It's even better if earnings rose faster than sales. The income statement also gives you a picture of the company's cash flow position. Cash flow consists of net profits plus depreciation. To arrive at a measurement of cash flow, divide the cash flow figure found in the statement by the amount of long-term debt. Anything under 20 percent is generally regarded as unsuitable—although there are exceptions.

Step Five

You should now turn to the profitability of the company. The margin of profit is determined by taking the operating income (i.e., income before payment of income tax) and dividing it by total sales. Certain industries, such as supermarket chains, have low profit margins—1 percent to 2 percent—whereas most industrial companies have margins in the neighborhood of 5 percent. Look for companies with stable and rising profit margins.

Step Six

The balance sheet, traditionally a two-page spread, contains the company's assets (everything the company owns) on the left and its liabilities (everything the company owes) on the right. Things that can quickly be converted into cash are called current assets, while the debts due within one year (which can be paid out of current assets) are called current liabilities. It is important to realize that the balance sheet offers the company's financial picture only at a single point in time. Like a snapshot, it gives you an instant idea of the corporation's strength. Its purpose is to show what the company owes and owns. Among the things to check are:

- How much cash is included under current assets. If the amount is shrinking, you must question what is draining this money from operations.

- The net working capital figure, a key number in determining a company's financial health. You can calculate this by subtracting current liabilities from current assets. This is what actually would be left over if all current debts were paid off; therefore it shows the resources available within the company to cover short-term debts. You can determine if this dollar amount is at a safe level by converting it into a ratio. Simply divide current assets by current liabilities to get the current asset-to-debt ratio. Most stock analysts like to see a 2:1 ratio. The net working captial is a crucial figure for investors to monitor, for if it drops there may not be sufficient money for expansion or future growth.

- The quick ratio, another means of determining financial strength, can be derived from the balance sheet. To arrive at this number, subtract inventories from current assets and divide by current liabilities. This figure should be more than one; in other words, current assets less inventories should at least be equal to if not exceed current liabilities. The quick ratio is a way to find out if a company is able to take care of its current debts as they mature.

- The company's ability to meet its obligations is another measure of financial strength. This, too, can be determined from the balance sheet by finding the debt-to-equity ratio. Divide long-term debt by total capitalization; both figures are generally given. (Total capitalization consists of long-term debt, common stock, capital surplus, retained earnings, and preferred stock.) A manufacturing company is in good shape if debt is 20 percent or less of capitalization. Higher debt ratios—40 percent to 50 percent—are acceptable in some industries, such as utilities. A high debt-to-equity ratio indicates that the company is probably borrowing to keep going—an acceptable position if sales are growing too and if there is an adequate amount of cash to meet payments. Beware, however, if sales start to fall, too.

There are many more sophisticated ratios you can obtain from working with the annual report, but these six steps are a good beginning. Don't forget to look for the elementary facts, too. They're just as important and include:

- The size of the company. What are its assets? A large company is less likely to face a sudden failure.

- The age of the company. Older firms have weathered good times and bad.

- The management. Are they experienced and are they personally investing in the company?

- The company's earnings. Are net earnings per share going up? Check the previous five years' record and look for trends in net sales, too.

There are other important indicators in the annual report. So for more extensive instruction on how to make sense out of the report, write to:

Merrill Lynch Pierce Fenner & Smith, Inc.
One Liberty Plaza
New York, NY 10080

for a copy of "How to Read a Financial Report."

The important thing to keep in mind is that you must compare these key indicators from one year to the next. Is the company's net working capital up or down? What is the trend in the changes in the debt-to-equity ratio? One year's statistics are not sufficient evidence on which to judge a company.